A Writer's Manual
11 Powerful ingredients to make you a Prolific Writer

Suniti Chandra Mishra

Published by:

F-2/16, Ansari Road, Daryaganj, New Delhi-110002
☎ 011-23240026, 011-23240027 • *Fax:* 011-23240028
Email: info@vspublishers.com • *Website:* www.vspublishers.com

Regional Office : Hyderabad
5-1-707/1, Brij Bhawan (Beside Central Bank of India Lane)
Bank Street, Koti, Hyderabad - 500 095
☎ 040-24737290
E-mail: vspublishershyd@gmail.com

Branch Office : Mumbai
Godown # 34 at The Model Co-Operative Housing, Society Ltd.,
"Sahakar Niwas", Ground Floor, Next to Sobo Central, Mumbai - 400 034
☎ 022-23510736
E-mail vspublishersmum@gmail.com

Follow us on:

All books available at **www.vspublishers.com**

© Copyright: Author
ISBN 978-81-920796-2-2
Edition 2011

The Copyright of this book, as well as all matter contained herein (including illustrations) rests with the Publisher. No person shall copy the name of the book, its title design, matter and illustrations in any form and in any language, totally or partially or in any form. Anybody doing so shall face legal action and will be responsible for damages.

Printed at : Param Offseters Okhla New Delhi-110020

Myriads of mystic tongues find utterance in one speech, and myriads of hidden mysteries are revealed in a single melody.

Baha'u'llah

Dedication

I affectionately dedicate this book to my children
Sneha, Shwetank and Shreya
as well as
all who are still 'children at heart',
who want to express their tender and
powerful thoughts.

Who knows the Secret of the Secrets?

What is the mystery behind a superb penmanship?
How were all the great books written?
How were the most splendid pieces of art carved out?
How is the genius revealed in a master work?
How are touching impressions made on the souls?

**if you don't know the answer already,
turn to the last page of this book ....**

Contents

The Publisher's Note	7
Author's Note - The Train	9
Heart-o-Meter	12
1. Read Before You Write	15
2. You and Your Writing	25
3. Connect to the Source	38
4. How Some Great Books were Written	51
5. Observe and Imagine	60
6. The Treasure of Silence	69
7. Gather Your Thoughts	81
8. Be 'Love-intoxicated'	96
9. Words can be 'Friends'	108
10. Infusing Life into Your Language	121
11. The Magic of 'AIDACADEBRA'	136
Two Prayers that will Help You Write Well	147
Answer to Exercise	150
Heart-o-Meter	162

THE PUBLISHER'S NOTE

Being a prominent publisher of utilitarian books, we have always attempted to bring the most useful sets of books for our keen readers. Our increasing popularity is testimonial to the fact that people trust in our quality as a caterer to their endless quest of knowledge.

This book is a new addition to the rich treasure of our top-ranking Self-help books. "How to write well" is a challenge that is faced not only by our young students but also working men and women. Whatever be your calling, you cannot escape this challenge! So why not to meet this challenge in a proficient way? There are many books out there which are nothing more than a compilation of letters, applications, etc. for different occasions. They may be very helpful but they cannot come to your aid on every occasion of life. This book is quite a different thing. It helps you become the MASTER of your own individual writing skill by following some simple and interesting rules. Every person can benefit from these rules based on his or her own personal interest, diligence, and persistence for acquiring a fine penmanship.

Another important feature is that each chapter is small in size so that it becomes interesting and not boring, memorable and not perplexing. TEN TOP TIPS given at the end of each chapter, followed by simple multi-optional Exercises to tune up your progress and creative Assignments that boost up your imagination further make this book an interesting tool in the hands of old and young readers alike.

Every step advised in this book is a scientific step to promote the learning skills of any person – young or old, student or professional. Yet, the subjects covered in this book are so comprehensive in nature that they do not only enhance your writing skills but even your general personality and outlook because, as it is rightly said, your writing and you are two inseparable entities. The simplicity of language of this book is an added feature that makes it a gospel of easy learning even for children and those whose proficiency in English is of beginners' level. Now with this unique book in your hand, your pen will glitter into gold. Congratulations in advance and wish you Happy Writing!

Author's Note

THE TRAIN

When I was a child, one of the many things that excited my imagination was a railway train. Its vibrant rustling noise would invite me near the track to fervently watch it run with a pace of fleeting time and leaving behind the throbbing impressions of a gone-by dream. My cousin, who was four years elder to me, often accompanied me. It was he who pointed to me how mighty was the engine that could pull the long train comprised of so many bogies. I know he was as wise as all other elders who, in their utter ignorance, impart a basically wrong knowledge into the minds of their inferiors. And I was as foolish as any other child of my age that even after watching the train-driver throwing coals into the big burning hole, could never realize that an engine has no power in itself to pull the train. It is the STEAM that makes miracles, and nowadays when steam-trains have ceased to be, the same role is being played by ELECTRICITY. The energy that actually pulls the train is, thus, far subtle, more powerful and yet hidden from our bare eyes.

For ages, our 'elders' have been teaching us that the fluency and potency in our writing comes by our sound knowledge of grammar, rich vocabulary and ample understanding of sentence structures. They are not wrong ... but once again, the glory of ENGINE is being sung and even though every careful student agrees to the fact that in spite of all grammatical and compositional tactics they have failed in writing even a paragraph of abiding impression, they have not been able to grasp the power actually being exercised by some hidden 'steam', some obscure 'electricity'.

The engine is very important for the running of a train because it has devices and receptacles to control and receive the power generated by steam or electricity but if there is no "power", then? A sound knowledge of grammar, a wonderful mastery in vocabulary, a deep understanding of syntax are all very important if one wants to improve one's writing but the power of writing comes from a simpler and subtler entity – a desire to write well.

This book is not written to threaten and intimidate the readers by giving them the wrong information that the engine pulls the train but to unburden their minds by rightly advising them that the 'power' to write well is within their grasp, in the reach of their own heart. This book deals with some basic, simple and genuinely tested 'elements' that foster the readers' desire in this direction and help them identify how to generate and regulate the 'power' that is behind a good writing.

This is not a tailor-made book available on book-shops in which to find a 'collection' of different letters, applications, essays and other 'marketable' write-ups in a 'pick-and-choose' manner. This is not a 'bank' of 'pre-written' materials for 'rush-and-carry' customers. This is a book that lovingly and systematically teaches you how to write anything easily and comfortably using your own knowledge and imagination. This is a self-help book for those who really feel that expressing things in an effective and touching way is all what they want.

Its mastermind approach makes it a profitable book for almost all sorts of learners – high school children, college students, office clerks and correspondents, housewives seeking self-learning, secretaries, content writers, press reporters, and anyone on this earth who thinks he or she is in a learning stage irrespective of age, gender, nationality, education or occupation.

This book will NOT make you a prolific writer or a talented penman unless you feel that urge and desire in your own heart. Great writers are born but good writers are made. Moreover, this one book in itself cannot guarantee your full success as a writer. First of all, there are many – and more scholarly and usefully written – books on this subject from renowned writers that you must read and, secondly, becoming a good writer is a continuous journey. No matter how many books you have read, you are still a learner.

This is just a capsule book which teaches you some most basic elements that make out a good writer and helps you intensify your desire to learn more by yourself. The interesting fact is that the greatest things in the universe are the simplest things. There should be no fear, no hesitation because you don't need so much 'knowledge' for writing than you need a 'desire' to say something. In this fun-filled journey, you will not only learn how to write well but also explore many hidden qualities of your own. THAT'S THE MAGIC OF THIS BOOK.

To reap the best of this book, BE A TRUE STUDENT! You need to follow every rule, every exercise. Even if you consider something very easy or 'not-important', do follow the rule, complete each Exercise, act on each Assignment. The psychology behind any serious achievement is complete obedience, submission, dedication, care and willingness to be patient and diligent. By following each exercise, you will be demonstrating these qualities and, hence, will be entitled to gain proficiency. All Assignments are not necessarily based on the information supplied in this book. They rather tend to encourage the students and readers to develop their own creativity and learn to find their own resources.

Almost all exercises are very easy. It does not mean you should overlook them. We should not expect that true knowledge comes only through rigorous and difficult pieces of information and mental stratagem. Knowledge, in its purity, is as simple as a child. Enjoy all the exercises and evaluate your own scores with the help of the ANSWER PAGE. Relish and act on them as a child, no matter you are a child in your 'teens' or in your 'ties'.

The book starts with a Heart-o-Meter and ends with the same. Please complete both the Heart-o-Meters. The Heart-o-Meter in the beginning tells you, by your own evaluation, where you are starting from – the level of your own writing skill judged by none other but YOU. As the texts will end, you will be able to re-measure your own progress by again completing the Heart-o-Meter in the end.

Remember, your writing expresses what YOU are. Such an important aspect of life cannot be left for chance. We hope this book will help bring the best in you and best out of you! Welcome to this exciting voyage!

— **Suniti Chandra Mishra**

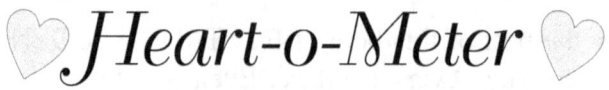 Heart-o-Meter

PLEASE DO NOT SKIP
THIS PART OF THE BOOK

Answer all the questions honestly (it means, tick mark only that which you really feel about yourself, not what you think is right or appropriate) and follow the self-scoring pattern to know your present writing skill level.

Q 1. I agree that:

- ☐ A. I can write almost on any normal topic with a short notice.
- ☐ B. I can write almost on any normal topic if I am given few days' time to prepare.
- ☐ C. It is very difficult for me to write on any topic, even if the topic is simple.
- ☐ D. I can never write easily on any topic.

Q 2. In my opinion, the most important thing for a successful writing is:

- ☐ A. clear idea
- ☐ B. right words
- ☐ C. good sentences
- ☐ D. style of writing

Q 3. Basically, a true writing is:

- ☐ A. something that should come from our heart.
- ☐ B. something which should reflect our intellect.
- ☐ C. something which should be logical.
- ☐ D. a nonsense; it's the worst art of expression.

Q 4. My most favourite writer is the one who/whose:

- ☐ A. books touch my heart and lead me to think something anew.
- ☐ B. teaches me some new skill.
- ☐ C. helps me to enrich my vocabulary by putting new words in his contents.
- ☐ D. books are always the best-sellers.

Q 5. Before I start writing:

- ☐ A. I calm my mind for some minutes and imagine and note down the basic outlines of the subject.
- ☐ B. I think a little and start.
- ☐ C. I just think on the first line and start.
- ☐ D. I just start writing.

Q 6. In my opinion, a good writing normally has the following qualities in order of importance:

- ☐ A. clarity, depth, beauty, brevity
- ☐ B. depth, clarity, beauty, brevity
- ☐ C. beauty, depth, clarity, brevity
- ☐ D. brevity, beauty, depth, clarity

Q 7. When I have to write something:

- ☐ A. words flow to me as I think and write.
- ☐ B. I sit with a dictionary and/or a thesaurus and choose the right words.
- ☐ C. I first write whatever comes and then rewrite everything in the end choosing the best words.
- ☐ D. I don't care for words. I just have to write somehow.

Q 8. I believe:

- ☐ A. in the power of my subconscious (inspirational) mind; it guides me through a powerful writing.

☐ B. in the power of my conscious (logical) mind; it guides me through a powerful writing.
☐ C. in good preparation on a vast range of topics; that's the key of success for a powerful writing.
☐ D. that there is nothing important about writing.

Q 9. I think that:

☐ A. I need to read a lot of good books to improve my writing.
☐ B. I need to read many books of my favourite writer to copy his or her style.
☐ C. a daily reading of newspaper is ideal for improving my writing.
☐ D. reading has nothing to do with my writing skill.

Q 10. I can write a 300 word paragraph on "The Goal of My Life" in:

☐ A. about 10 minutes.
☐ B. about 15 minutes
☐ C. about 20 minutes
☐ D. I don't know

Now that you've honestly answered each question, score yourself as follows:

- For each 'A' you have ticked, give yourself 4 marks.
- For each 'B' you have ticked, give yourself 3 marks.
- For each 'C' you have ticked, give yourself 2 marks.
- For each 'D' you have ticked, give yourself 1 mark.

☐ 36-40 = Very Good   ☐ 32-35 = Good
☐ 28-31 = Average   ☐ Below 28 = Poor

Chapter 1

Read Before You Write

Reading maketh a full man, conference a ready man, and writing an exact man.

- Sir Francis Bacon

Reading, conference and writing make the foundation-stone of the world of knowledge, three vistas through which we can peek into a panoramic universe hitherto unknown. Without reading, there can be no knowledge. Of course, in the history of humankind, there have been people who were not 'well-read' and yet they possessed immense knowledge. If you look into the life of the personalities such as Saint Kabirdas, Joan of Arc, William Shakespeare, Tagore, Kalidas, and hosts of other men of letters in the areas of science, industries, arts and literature, politics and economics and so on, this will hold true for all of them. You will see that many of them did not 'read' even high school books and yet they imparted matchless knowledge and insight to the human world.

No Knowledge without 'Reading' ....

The Microsoft Chairman and one of the richest persons of the world, **Bill Gates**, does not hold a 'great' academic background. The engineers working under him are far more educated than him. Similar is the story of **Michael Dell**, founder of Dell, Inc. – a company famous for its laptops – who did not complete his college. **Henry Ford** fulfilled his dream of making "horseless" carts by making Ford Motors a worldwide success, but he too did not succeed in acquiring a high school degree. A figure parallel to Ford who, too, became a legendary man was **Rockefeller**. Stepping into his shoes, India's **Dhirubhai Ambani**, the founder of Reliance Industries, made an empire from scratch. Both were sparely educated. One of the richest men in Russia, **Roman Abramovich**, was a college drop out. Many successful actors and actresses of the world of cinema, including **Halle Berry, Meena Kumari, Anthony Andrews, Jack Albertson, Woody Allen, Ben Affleck, Tom Hanks, Dilip Kumar, Marilyn Monroe, Julie Andrews, Jennifer Aniston** and (the list is endless..) .... did not have any mentionable educational background. Another striking example is that of **Mark Zuckerberg**, the founder of the famous social networking site Facebook. He is one of the youngest Billionaires on the Forbes' list. Though he's not highly educated, his idea of Facebook tipped him to join the rank of 400 richest people in USA. Many writers, such as **Hans Christian Anderson**, who became shining stars of the literary firmament, never had proper schooling. **Rabindra Nath Tagore**, the Nobel Prize winner poet laureate of India, used to escape from school and play out with children. Several sportsmen such as **Andre Agassi** and **Sachin Tendulkar** had no worthwhile schooling. Many scientists were no exception. **Albert Einstein**, considered to be a genius of all times, was nothing but a child "***mentally slow, unsociable and adrift forever in his foolish dreams***", according to his teacher. **Thomas Alva Edison**, the most renowned of all scientists for his hundreds of useful inventions, had a hearing problem, was scoffed by his classmates, and had to leave school.

This is not even a fraction of the entire list of great people who never received any formal education. Some of them could not even 'read' an alphabet. Thus, it means that 'reading' does not mean reading 'books' only. It is said that each event has a story to tell, each atom has treasures inside it. Even though these successful people, as mentioned above, did not 'read' so many books, they did 'read' more important things of life. They 'read' human hearts, they 'read' the hidden principles of success, they 'read' the laws of nature, they 'read' the ups and downs of life and abstracted the clandestine 'mantras' of the inner power. So, do you understand now that without reading there can be no knowledge? If you want to be a good writer, READ everything ... every person ... every object ... every character ... every face ... every tear ... every smile ... everything that attracts you.

Reading is like a Receptionist ...

However, in a general sense, reading applies to reading of books. The first thing to know in this connection is that whatever we read, occupies the 'outer level' of our mind. When we visit an office, the first establishment we come across is a small but attractive 'Reception' area. The Receptionist has <u>all the information</u> to be able to respond to your basic queries – where to go for a certain work, whom to meet, what are the procedures, and all sorts of important things! The Receptionist may not be able to give you probably detailed or 'in-depth' answers, for which, you may have to go and meet the right officials.

Reading is like a Receptionist, sitting somewhere in the outer area of the mind who knows the basics of many things. <u>Reading can guide you but it alone cannot give you profound knowledge and insight. It only</u>

activates the 'information centre' of the mind. Thus, *"reading maketh a full man"* – full with information and references!

Howbeit, reading and writing are closely associated with each other. The more you read, the better you can write. Allan W. Eckert said: *"**If you'd be a writer, first be a reader. Only through the assimilation of ideas, thoughts and philosophies can one begin to focus his own ideas, thoughts and philosophies.**"* Thus, the role of reading is very clear and can be summed up as follows:

- Reading gives us facts and information which become the base of our writing.
- When we read, our mind becomes influenced and is shaped along the thoughts of the writer. Sometimes, these thoughts have a lifelong influence on us and they make our 'core values'. That's why it is important to be careful of what we are reading.
- When we read different writers, different thought-patterns are imbibed in our mind. To accept some of these thoughts and refuse or neutralize others, our mind assumes an active role. Thus, our own rational power grows and our individual thoughts and principles are crystallized.
- What we read most, we become. If a person is always in the books of fantasies, his life also takes the shape of fantasy in itself.
- The more we read, the more do we become familiar with better expressions, arguments, styles and structures and they all together enrich our writing.

What is 'Active Reading'?

When reading is an important factor in making successful writers, it must be given <u>planned attention</u> in the life of every student -- children and youth in particular because they can truly enjoy reading. They are also receptive and curious and if they choose good books, their fertile minds will soon become a '*Greenland*' of wonderful ideas, imaginations and thoughts that will change the world.

A planned attention on reading means doing active reading. When you read actively, you must follow these four steps:

1. You can observe the style of a particular writer and if you come across some beautiful, appealing expressions you can pen them

down in a notebook. Later, you can write several sentences of your own on the same pattern. For example, take this oft-quoted line of Jeanne Manon Philipon (better known as Madame Roland): "***O Liberty! What crimes are committed in thy name!***" See, how "Liberty" has been personified and has been associated with an irony (crime committed in her name). Or observe this piece of a poem of Surdas, a Hindi poet: "***O Krishna, Why you go to play so far? Today, I heard, a bugaboo has come in the jungle, you don't know, My Child!***" (*Khelat door jaat kit kanha ... aaj sunyo ban haoo ayo tu nahi janat nanha*). See, how Krishna's mother alarms him to keep away from going far! Observe the simplicity and beauty of motherly love! According to your aptitude, many such expressions can be striking to you.

2. You may also develop a special aptitude for a particular writer and thus read lots of books of that very writer. In this way, that writer becomes your 'Role Model in Writing', so to say, and even without knowing you start reflecting his or her style, thoughts and modes of expression. <u>In the beginning, it may seem like imitation, but gradually your own individuality will crystallize.</u> Eventually, your own 'class' is created, your personal thoughts are solidified and your own unique character as a writer will begin to take shape. It will be worthwhile to note here, that this role model approach is almost essential and natural for everyone who has become a man of essence in any field. Name any striking sports star and you can find his source of inspiration in a player of the past. Every great writer bloomed by getting inspiration form another great writer. This is a process and not an imitation. It becomes imitation only when the person does not learn anything, does not let his own personality grow, and, naturally, in that case, he never becomes anything.

3. Try to go beyond your selected reading and try to read something that you earlier did not care for. It means trying a new subject you were not very interested in but which is not distasteful, too. For example, earlier may be you always liked to read fiction. You also have a favourite writer in this area whom you appreciate and who has become your 'Role Model in Writing'. However, in this third step of active reading you choose, to read something different, say, a non-fiction book or a motivational book of some kind. You

usually don't enjoy reading non-fiction but they are not a taboo for you as well. <u>When we dare to read beyond our 'favourite' area, we expand our mind and its attitudinal dimensions</u>. We learn new vocabularies and terminologies, new ways of expressions.

4. When the third stage passes, active reading takes you to a more difficult but versatile level of reading. Even though no writer can be a 'Jack of all trades' and, it is true, that every writer specializes in his or her own area, there is no harm in expanding our horizon of knowledge and see if new thoughts, new jargons, new phrases and slangs enrich our writing. To this effect, sometimes - if not often - every person who yearns to be an empowered writer must tread beyond his 'comfort zone' and try to read something 'contrary to his taste'. For example, maybe you have no interest at all in science fiction or a sport-related article, to be versatile, you must digest diversities. For this reason, you may do a favour to yourself and dedicate at least a day in a month to read a book 'contrary to your taste'. In this way, you will master more insipid words, learn more diverse syntaxes and, above all, <u>you will be able to expand your mind to incorporate thoughts and information from additional areas of life.</u>

The keynote to remember is that diversity in reading brings diversity in writing. In brief, active reading involves two types of reading – <u>Choice Reading</u> and <u>Forced Reading</u>. Choice helps to develop your inherent qualities, and Forced Reading expands your mind to be able to respond to writing needs often demanded by an occasion, such as examinations, news reporting, etc. Students appearing for regular school examinations or selected exams like IELTS, TOEFL, etc., do not always have to write on subjects of their choice. They have to be able to express their ideas on diverse topics, not necessarily evoking their interest. It is through FORCED READING that one can develop penmanship often demanded by these crucial exams.

Reading evokes imagination...

Another important benefit of reading is that it evokes our imagination. Each writer is a creator. He or she ushers us into a new world hitherto unknown. For example, in her famous **Harry Potter** books, J.K. Rowling takes you to the magical world which was unimaginable to you before.

Alice in Wonderland, Gulliver's Travels, The Panchatantra – all reveal to us a unique world characterized by their own respective phenomenal auras and ambiences. When you read, you imagine and imagination is the best friend of the writers.

Furthermore, as we keep on reading, we come across myriads of personalities and, in a way, interact with them. Great characters such as Hamlet, Devdas, Sindabad, Arjuna, Hanuman, Shantanu, Izmeralda, Lucy, Ali Baba, Hatim Tai, Hercules, Max Demian and so many others have not just meant to us as imaginary characters of poetry, drama or fiction but they occupy a special corner in our heart. We think of them, sympathize with them, make them our heroes or heroines, we see our own image in their eminent personalities. In this way, we 'co-relate' with the emotions and feelings of others, and this susceptibility is a vital property for all writers.

Shun television and movies; don't kill your imagination…

Long before the age of television and cinema, people were simply fond of reading. Whether they were in the trains, in trams or buses, in their bed-room or study room, people who often seen holding a book in their hands, reading and imagining the characters that were described. If they were reading the story of Krishna, the reader had his own unique image of Krishna in his mind. If it was the brave Sindbad the sailor, they were well imagining his adventurous spirit, his traits and qualities along the pages they were turning curiously. A serious and complex character like Shakespeare's Hamlet, for grown-up readers, was visualized in their own mind's aptitudes and dimensions, coloured according to each reader's personal tastes and tints. Sharat Chandra's tragic-romantic character, Devdas, used to be a unique personality for the keen readers.

Then everything changed. A director appeared and 'moulded' Krishna and His greatness in an imitative and often ridiculous role of a mortal hero who could be anyone ranging from Dhriti Bhatia to Meghan Jadhav or from Swapnil Joshi to Sarvadaman Banerjee. Now, especially for children, Krishna can never re-appear in His original greatness as visualized in their unprejudiced minds. Whenever they will close their eyes to see that divine beauty, a Nitish Bhardwaj will smile. And, may be, in one of these 'glimpses', Lord Krishna will also be contesting an election! A bunch of other film-makers sprang up to show the dualism and hesitation, skepticism and inner conflict, shock and trauma of Hamlet in over dozens of versions though none of them – including Laurence Olivier, Edwin Booth or Morris Hunt -- could be as perfect as a reader's own view in his mind of Hamlet. In a similar manner, Devdas that we see in the Indian cinema deprives us from *individually* imagining and understanding the real pains and tragedies that a character of Sharat Chandra could have suffered. From Phani Sharma to K.L. Saigal and from Dilip Kumar to Shahrukh Khan and Zara Shaikh, no one can match the true Devdas that he really was or could be for each individual reader. Sindbad's real personality was replaced by a Douglas Fairbanks or another like him and the same happened with many immortal characters that could mean something else for us but were 'imposed' on our minds as a different, limited, stunted personalities 'carved out' by a cinema or television tycoon.

This is not to say that television and cinema should be banned or that they are useless. It is also agreeable that in many cases the film version of a story have proved to be more influential than the real story itself. The purpose is only to outline the fact that when we read, our imagination is set free and it colours the characters and places, events and emotions according to our own inner conceptions. At the same time, another reader has a different conception. Our imaginative skills are developed. Our mind uses its own canvas, its own palettes and hues, its own brushes and blends. However, when we watch a television show or a movie, our freedom of creativity is taken away by a clever plot. Our canvas and palettes are snatched away. We are given coloured specks to wear and see the characters as the directors would like us to see. If you will consider this condition with regard to children, who are easily influenced by the way things are presented to them, you will appreciate the type of serious 'mental killing' it is! A new word should be coined – *imaginicide* – as these mediums of entertainment are truly killing the imaginations a child could have.

Ample focus on reading is the only remedy to prevent this *Imaginicide*.

The benefits of reading are manifold. It is sufficient to say that reading is a two-dimensional journey at the same time – a journey to the outer world, the world of knowledge and information and also a journey within yourself, exploring your own likes and dislikes, strengths and weaknesses.

Ten Top Tips

1. Reading, conference (discussion) and writing are three basics or three dimensions – of knowledge.

2. Reading is essential for knowledge but it does not mean reading books only. 'Reading' means acquiring knowledge from everything and everyone.

3. Whatever we read occupies the outer level of our mind and enriches our information.

4. What we read most, we become.

5. The more we read, the better we can write.

6. Reading influences our minds. We learn better expressions, arguments, styles and structures and they all together enrich our writing.

7. When we pay planned attention on reading, it is known as active reading and it comprises of four stages.

8. Active reading involves two types of reading – choice reading and forced reading.

9. Diversity in reading brings diversity in writing.

10. Reading evokes our imagination and helps to 'co-relate' with the emotions and feelings of others.

Exercise 1

Match your answers with those given on the ANSWER PAGE. Give yourself 2 marks for each correct answer.

1. **What are the three dimensions of knowledge?**
   A. Reading, Writing and Arithmetic
   B. Reading, Reporting and Revising
   C. Reading, Writing and Conference
   D. Remembering, Revising and Re-writing

2. **The word "reading", in its true sense, implies:**
   A. Reading only the books of knowledge
   B. Reading everything else but books
   C. Reading the science of handwriting or palmistry, etc.,
   D. Reading books as well as learning from everything

3. **Reading is like a _____, sitting somewhere in the outer area of the mind and knowing the basics of many things.**
   A. Receptionist   B. Guide
   C. Officer   D. Minister

4. **In what way "reading and writing are closely associated with each other"?**
   A. The less we read, the more we write.
   B. The less we read, the better we can write.
   C. The more we read, the less we write.
   D. The more we read, the better we can write.

5. **Why is it important to be careful of what we are reading?**
   A. Because too much reading explodes us with unwanted information.
   B. Because all that we read have an influence on our mind and they make our 'core values'.
   C. Because reading different writers makes us 'split' personalities.
   D. Because reading exposes us to worlds hitherto unknown.

6. **Which one is NOT true about active reading?**
   A. We carefully observe the style of a particular writer and note down important things.
   B. We make a particular author our "Role Model in Writing".
   C. We also plan to read such books as we do not generally like or prefer.
   D. We only do 'forced reading' to expand our mind's dimensions.

Assignments 1

1. Write a short paragraph (maximum 500 words) on the **most impressive book** you ever read. (*Model answer given on the ANSWER PAGE*)

2. Who is your most favourite or '**Role Model**' writer? Write about him or her in about 200 words and why he or she is your favourite writer? (*Model answer given on the ANSWER PAGE*)

3. If you are asked to give **your list** of **10 most successful people** in the world, who will be there on your list? Write against each of them (*in one sentence*) why you consider him or her to be successful?

MY LIST OF 10 MOST SUCCESSFUL PEOPLE	WHY I CONSIDER HIM/HER TO BE SUCCESSFUL

4. Write 10 beautiful expressions (sentences) from any good book you are currently reading.

5. Make a list of 3 primary (favourite) topics on which you would <u>like</u> to read a book. Make a list of 3 secondary topics on which you would <u>like</u> to read a book. Make a list of 3 tertiary topics on which you would <u>not like</u> to read a book.

Chapter 2

You and Your Writing

> *Only write from your own passion, your own truth. That's the only thing you really know about. Anything else leads you away from the pulse.*
>
> – Marianne Williamson

Mind is a creative faculty of a human being. It thinks and continues to think. In a day, not less than some 50000 ideas pass through our mind – some of them weak and some of them strong. When an idea is strong or overwhelming, one is naturally compelled to express it in some way, and writing is the most impressive way of all expressions. That is how all the world's literature developed. Writing is truly a gift of God to mankind.

The Growing Significance of Writing for People...

With the explosion of the information age in which we are living now, and the expansion of knowledge and education, more and more strong and overflowing ideas are springing forth in human minds and far sweeter songs have started echoing in the hearts of men and women of today. The role of writing has scaled above the normal heights of artistic and literary expressions. Today, no matter who and where we are, in whatever profession we have engaged ourselves, there's no escape from writing. In fact, in today's knowledge-based world, much of your success depends on your writing efficiency. As a student, you have to face examinations and project assignments; as an office-worker, you have to cope with daily reports, memorandums and official letters; as a business man, you have to launch products using the most yielding words and project the features of your services to make them more appealing and inviting; as an individual, you have to develop rapport with your friends and maintain a vibrant social relationship often using various modes of writing, emails and formal letters, etc.

- If you can write well, you can attract more friends, clients and customers. If not, you will lose them.
- If you can write efficiently, you will feel confident. If not, you will feel like a mediocre who hardly exists.

- If you can write powerfully, you will emit a clear signal to all that you are a powerful person. If your writing is not impressive, nobody will count on you.

- If you can write clearly, vividly and expressively, people will trust you and your services, because they will have a clear idea about you. On the other hand, ineffective writing keeps you in a 'hidden pavilion' and nobody will know who you are.

So important is Writing that it is incumbent upon everyone to learn and master this art to scale even greater heights of success.

The previous chapter dealt with the importance of reading as a vital aspect for learning the art of writing. While reading provides us with conscious wisdom, writing is a way to subconsciously tap the knowledge acquired by reading. When you write, you are in touch with a deeper section of the mind. You are activating your brain-cells that are far inside the so-called 'reception' or 'information' area. Try to prove it to yourself! Read this paragraph aloud and notice how your mind is involved in reading. While reading, were you able to entertain some other thoughts? While reading, could you easily notice the people, the sounds, the scenery, the fragrance around you? What is you answer? YES ... of course! While reading, countless cells of your brain were free to observe and perceive other objects around you. While reading, your mind travels beyond your surrounding area and roams anywhere, imagines many things.

Now take a pen and a piece of paper and write down the above paragraph or write a paragraph of your own. FINISH THIS FIRST. ..... What did you observe? Was your mind as free as it was when you were reading? Could you notice, observe or perceive as many things as you did when you were reading?

Writing: A Deeper Business of the Mind...

This simple experiment clearly testifies that writing is a deeper business of mind than reading. It involves more brain-cells, requires more attention, more energy.

When you read, you are dealing with your conscious mind, your logical mind, your apparent mind – and this mind has a limited power which is hardly 5% of the total mind power. When you write something from the depth of your heart, you are connected to your subconscious mind, your miraculous mind, your latent mind – and this mind has unlimited power. A person can benefit from this limitless subconscious capacity of the mind in proportion to his or her own personal receptivity and willingness. In this way, writing takes you steps ahead, and makes you an exact man as you are.

In writing, you are in close touch with yourself. Since writing has to deal with your subconscious nature, 'you' just become <u>you</u> when you write. You can deceive the whole world but you cannot deceive yourself. Your writing will bring out your real self, howsoever you hide ..... subconsciously!

The Veteran Russian Spy...

There was a veteran Russian spy who was in a European country on a high diplomatic mission. He was an expert detective and could change his appearance and traits by using a number of masks, applying different cosmetics, wearing all sorts of European dresses and speaking at least 10 major languages of the world. The European detectives suspected him but he eluded them and also held a position so high that they could not arrest him without being sure that he was a Russian.

Then a trick was played on this Russian spy. When all were in a party, an officer hurried to him and said: "***Sir, I'm sorry but your beloved wife just died in a car accident!***". "*Это не возможно. Я разговаривал с ней только сейчас*" ("It is not possible. I talked to her just now.") – He yelled in Russian and was immediately handcuffed by the police. Your condition when you are writing is not different from that Russian spy who could not overcome his 'real self' in a subconscious moment.

Your Writing is You ...

When we are in our 'natural' state of shock, grief, wonder, joy, etc., we act subconsciously and reveal our origin. In writing, too, we are connected to our original self. We can be any thing on this planet but our writing ultimately reveals our <u>exact</u> nature. There's no exception to this rule! There is a solid science based on the study of handwriting. Your handwriting or calligraphy displays your personality. The one who is versed in this science can tell – from every stroke, every bend, every curve, every slant of your letter – if you are a criminal or a saint. A reader, who is voracious and versatile, can tell – from every phrase, every syntax, every expression of your writing – the kind of person you are!

Such a significant thing is writing! Your writing is what you are! When you'll change, your writing will change. This is like the relationship between a shadow and its object!

Conference maketh a ready man ...

A student who only reads, only crams his or her lessons and does not write, does not make notes of important ideas he or she learnt, is using only 5% limited capacity of the brain. Naturally, the success ratio will also be only 5%. Conference enables us to ground our knowledge further. *'Conference maketh a ready man'* because it is like storming up our ideas and acquired knowledge by discussion. The dictionary meaning of 'conference' is: 'a meeting for consultation, exchange of information, or discussion'. In the world of knowledge, it implies a far more expanded dimension. It means 'intellectual meeting and consultation' with friends or people but it also refers to 'a meting with our own deep-rooted self' – a consultation within our own inner realm.

Conference helps us find new ideas and correlate all the pieces of information. The great Greek philosopher, Socrates, for example, was a curious child from the very beginning. His mind was always full of questions, and he would often run to the streets and suddenly grab the hand of an elderly person and ask: *"Can you tell me why it is so?"*

The 3-D World of Knowledge...

A good student reads a lot, then discusses the matters with his friends and teachers and notes down all that he or she has learnt in this three-fold process. This is the three-dimensional world of true knowledge. Those who are not school students are also, 'students' in the university of life and even when we are in the grave, it is a class-room of life. So the rule applies to all equally.

When we contemplate on something in our own heart, it is also a 'conference' with our own self. This has no less benefit than discussing the matter with someone else. This, in turn, promotes our interest to read more, discuss more and write more. Thus, this three-dimensional journey perpetually takes us to newer and yet newer heights of knowledge.

Inner Treasures of the Mind ...

Writing has its place in this three-dimensional world of knowledge. It helps us import all information we have received through reading. It helps us combine all the ideas we gained through discussion and then 'binds' them all together, so firmly that our knowledge and perception becomes solid and intact. It also helps us to connect our individual self with an ever-expanding world of knowledge. Thus, we become what we write. Thought is power. If it is true (and it is), then written thought is many times more powerful than spoken thought. So, why not acquire this miraculous power of thought?

Writing activates your brain-cells into deeper meanings of things and facts. This is done by tapping your subconscious capacities. These subconscious capacities yield you service in a natural way (*see next chapter: "Connect To the Source"*). You don't have to try anything. As you start writing, the subconscious power is automatically activated. It will be useful for you to know at this point how the subconscious mind helps us in writing.

1. The first thing is that the subconscious mind <u>forgets nothing</u>. It is the wonderful and amazing power of the mind that we often experience in our lives. Even if it is a face we saw some 50 years before, an event we encountered decades ago and even though normally we never remember them, the subconscious mind never forgets, it has a record and retrieval system far beyond the capacities of the best computers of the world. When you write, this amazing capacity starts working and you will be helped to remember old memories, faces, quotations, expressions, things you read, incidents you passed by and everything that is required for you. However, you have to be deeply occupied in your writing to take advantage of this miraculous power of the mind.

2. Secondly, the subconscious mind is your faithful servant during engrossed writing and in moments of deep reflection and meditation. It supports whatever idea you impress upon your mind and brings a hundred proofs and arguments to help you elaborate on your idea. But if you change your idea, it has another hundred proofs and arguments to support that new idea, too. **Consider this story of Akbar and Birbal to know your exact relationship with the subconscious mind.** When king Akbar was once dining with his minister, Birbal, the royal

cook served a nice preparation of brinjal which the king liked so much and praised brinjal as a very good vegetable. *"Of course it is the king of all vegetables"*, Birbal tweeted, *"that's why it has a crown on its head."* Days passed by and once again Akbar and Birbal were together for a lunch and once again brinjal was cooked …. but not so very tasty this time. Akbar made his mouth and said: *"Now I don't want this vegetable ever in my dish, it is so bad."* *"Sure it is"*, Birbal attuned his comment, *"that is why it is so ugly and shapeless"*. Akbar suddenly remembered Birbal's previous comment and ridiculed him for having such changed opinion on brinjal, but Birbal replied: *"Sir, I am your servant and not of the brinjal, your opinion is my opinion."* The subconscious mind has to tell us the same thing: *"your opinion is my opinion"* and it will leave no stone unturned to support you when you want to expatiate an idea.

3. Apart from its own illimitable memory to support you from your own experiences, reminiscences and knowledge of the past, the subconscious mind is a free channel linking your objective mind to the great subjective mind of the God or universe whatever you say. Thus, if you rely on it, it can bring such knowledge and wisdom to your service that could not – by any means - be imported by your limited mind.

The more you practice, the more profuse the revelations of the mind's inner treasures. Gradually, writing gives birth to a new germ in your mind – curiosity for the expansion of self – something that is the real purport of the supreme mind.

By not writing, I am committing a sin...

Any person, in any walk of life – retired or in service, professional or amateur, housewife or working, young or old – who is satisfied only reading the horrible newspapers daily which report all negative episodes of life or other books of any value or importance – is doing a sin to his or her own self if he or she does not write at least one page daily. By not writing, I want to say that *'I don't want to explore the best in me'*, and thus, I want to say that *'I am not concerned with what God wants to reveal through me'*.

When we write – even if a page of a diary every night before retiring, a poem, a thought paragraph, an idea, a story or whatever from our heart – we are allowing God, through our subconscious mind, to direct our footsteps to the next stairs of knowledge where we can 'express' something God wants to express through us. Otherwise, how will He speak if not through His own channels as we are!

Writings that changed the world...

Hesitation and self-underestimation is a normal part of human nature. Most people who have even a little flavour or desire for writing are introvert. They feel their writings will not be welcomed by people. Thus was the famous Austrian writer **Franz Kafka** who was so hesitant about his stories and novels that he never got them published in his lifetime and, before his death, asked his friend and manager, Max Brod, to destroy his writings without reading them. But Max published them and Franz Kafka became an immortal writer. Do you still want to hesitate and underestimate your writing?

And can you guess the name of a great world-moving fiction that is translated into more than 100 languages of the world, and which inspired dozens of films and animations? Will you believe that such an influential book was written by its author, **Lewis Carroll**, just to please a small bored girl named Alice Liddell? Can't guess still? The name of this book is **Alice in Wonderland**. Yet, will you dare to suppress the writer inside you?

If you are a simple housewife with responsibilities of children and household, may be not very educated, you may derive inspiration from the great Nobel Prize winner writer **Pearl S. Buck**. Soon after her first marriage, she bore a mentally retarded girl child, Carol. The situation of this girl filled this woman with love for children and it is said that most children stories that Pearl S. Buck wrote were designed to help Carol. And they became world classics. Have you ever thought about writing for your own children in case if you have any? Who knows a Pearl S. Buck may be lying hidden inside you!

You may be a young boy or a girl spending your vacations, or a man often bored in his free times. Did you not know how a great book of all times, often referred to as "the first modern novel" was written by a similarly bored person spending his time in a jail? What was worse, he had even lost one hand in a war. Yet he preferred to kill his boredom by writing something than worrying and lamenting on his melancholy condition. This man was **Miguel de Cervantes** – great Spanish writer – and his book **Don Quixote**. Will you still grieve that you have no time and facility?

Many busy people – as lofty in the rank as **George Washington**, the first President of America – stole tiny moments from their tea and coffee breaks and completed a book by writing a few paragraphs daily. And you say you are a busy office executive? Busier than **Jawahar Lal Nehru**, the first Prime Minister of India, who is not known only for his statesmanship but also for his great books like **The Discovery of India**?

You may be a simple reporter in a newspaper but if you will write imaginatively, you may become another **Hunter Thompson** who was asked to write a report on a motorcycle race but it proved to be a great American classic – **Fear and Loathing in Las Vegas** -- also made into a famous film.

Emily Dickinson was considered as an eccentric who lived in her own loneliness, spending time amidst plants and flowers. When her poems were published, her greatness was revealed. Same happened with Jane Austen, the world-renowned author of **Sense and sensibility, Pride and Prejudice, Emma**, and other books, who never gave any serious attention to bringing out her books in her lifetime, but became famous after her death.

In the famous Topkapi Palace Museum (Istanbul) there is a priceless 86-carat pear-shaped diamond. The story goes that this valuable diamond was originally found by a poor Turkish fisherman in whose opinion this was only a shining stone. He sold it to a jeweler just for three spoons and thus this diamond came to be named as the Spoon maker's Diamond. Each one of us may have inside us great thoughts and unforgettable stories, novel ideas and momentous expressions of some kind, though we may be hesitant and consider them trivial. Let's not be like that foolish fisherman.

'Forced' Writing...

Every art comes by practice .... so is writing. In the previous chapter, we talked about 'forced reading'. 'Forced writing' is also an equally important thing. If you are an aspiring writer or simply a student or a learner, the first thing you have to do is to 'discipline your mind and expand its capacities'.

Remember your childhood? How was it when you learnt to write the first letter of your alphabet ... the 'A' or its equivalent? You did not want to write ... you did not want to learn anything but the first tender teacher – usually your mother – 'forced' the pencil between your fingers, guided you through those 'standing' and 'sleeping' lines, those curves and crooks, which were so difficult and annoying for you, but you ultimately mastered and learnt all the letters of the alphabet ... with patience and perseverance ... with a 'forced' session of knowledge. In the same way, if you want to be a good writer, discipline yourself to write at least a paragraph daily. In the beginning, things may not come from the heart but then your own success will delight you and your writing will start to flow from the core. But if you procrastinate and wait that an inspiration should come from your heart and then you will pick up your pen, you will have wasted away a priceless learning time of your life.

Diary writing...

Daily diary writing is a good practice to this effect. Developing this habit has many benefits:

- You have to write it daily and, fortunately, diary writing is not forced writing. It is quite an enjoyable job.
- In a diary, you usually write about things that touch your heart, influence you or concern you. Thus, being a very personalized writing, it flows from your heart.
- Diary writing also provides an opportunity to track our own intellectual development, things that are playing a vital role in shaping our mind. Thus, we can know what influences are determining our subconscious thoughts and, accordingly, we can have control over them.

The important thing is that you should write, write and write. If you feel others will laugh at your writing, write and throw it out of the window, but write. A true writer writes for his or her own delight and not for approval of others. So write, write, and write. You may have a limited vocabulary, agreed that your knowledge of grammar is poor, possibly you are not confident, may be your spelling is too bad, but remember that the only answer to all these problems is – WRITE, WRITE, and WRITE. Those who keep writing, even if they are dull writers in the beginning, become a bright writer eventually. Those who don't write regularly, even if their talent is dazzling, will become a dull star in a corner one day.

Write it from your heart...

'Forced' writing does not mean that you should write insipid and tasteless things, coming forcefully out of your dry mind. It simply means 'disciplining' yourself by committing to daily writing. It is an initial stage and should soon lead you to writing from the heart.

If you truly have a desire to write, start writing now. This is the simplest method for becoming a good writer. Write about whatever touches you. Don't think what others will think. Be loyal to yourself and not to others. Go and trace the records of all good and great writers. They wrote for their own delight, they were honest with their own feelings. They were not cobblers preparing shoes of different sizes for customers.

Go and see the records of all unsuccessful or short-timed writers. They prepared shoes on orders. Don't be a customized writer. Follow your heart. If a flower blooms and it touches your heart, do write something on it. If the city is on fire and you have no feelings, forget it, and don't trouble your pen.

What did I say? Did I mean that a good writer is selfish? Is he or she concerned only with his own pains and pleasures? No, I simply meant that a true writer is not a hypocrite. He writes what he feels. However, to reach this level of feeling and this intensity of depth, a writer necessarily becomes a 'universal being'. That is, his or her feelings, though quite personal and individual, are so deep and general that they become the feelings of the multitude. When William Wordsworth tells us about the sad plight of Lucy, it is his personal emotion for Lucy but this emotion is so sublime that whosoever reads his poems, feels the same emotions for Lucy. William Wordsworth intentionally did not write to arouse the same feelings for Lucy in people's hearts. A musician composes an aching symphony that brings tears in the eyes of millions because the sublimity and intensity of the pain touched each and all. The musician 'intentionally' did not 'conspire' to bring tears in people's eyes.

Remember, if you can truly laugh at your writing, the whole world can laugh. If your writings can bring tears in your own eyes, their pensive effect will touch almost all human hearts. So write what YOU feel truly, and trust that your genuine feelings will be reflected in all – THIS IS THE FIRST LESSON FOR EVERY WRITER.

Ten Top Tips

1. When we read we use our conscious mind which has only 5% of the total mind power. When we write, we are tapping our subconscious mind which has unlimited capacities.
2. Your writing reveals your inner personality.
3. When you write, you subconsciously gain direction into the newer worlds of knowledge.
4. God wants to express something through each one of us – writing is one of the ways of this divine expression.
5. Writing gives birth to a new germ in your mind – curiosity for expansion of self.
6. READ to acquire knowledge, DISCUSS (or contemplate) to explore knowledge, WRITE to solidify knowledge.
7. It is a sacred duty of every person to write something daily.
8. Like 'forced' reading, the skill of writing can also be initially developed by 'forced' writing.
9. Daily diary writing has many benefits.
10. A true writer writes for himself or herself and not for others.

Exercise 2

Match your answers with those given on the ANSWER PAGE. Give yourself 2 marks for each correct answer.

1. When we write, we are connected to our _____ mind which has unlimited power.
   - A. Conscious
   - B. Subconscious
   - C. Unconscious
   - D. Super Conscious

2. What does this Russian sentence mean: "Это не возможно"?
   - A. I can do it
   - B. It's not possible
   - C. It's truly possible
   - D. There's nothing impossible

3. Which sentence is NOT true?
   - A. When you will change, your writing will change.
   - B. When you write, you gain direction into your inner self.
   - C. The power of the conscious mind is unlimited.
   - D. A good student notes down important points after reading.

4. How does 'conference' (talking with friends or contemplating in our own heart on a given subject) help us become a ready man?
   - A. By storming our knowledge to find newer ideas and correlate all the pieces of knowledge.
   - B. By dealing with our conscious mind.
   - C. By encouraging social networking.
   - D. By activating our subconscious capacities.

5. Though good writing must always come from heart, why should we 'force' ourselves to write everyday?
   - A. To discipline our mind and expand its capacities.
   - B. To learn new words and sentences.
   - C. Because whatever we write, will become a great writing.
   - D. Because this is a rule of thumb.

6. What is NOT true?
   - A. Diary writing is not a forced writing.
   - B. Diary writing is a very personalized writing.
   - C. Diary writing helps us to track and control the things influencing our mind.
   - D. Diary writing usually deals with our daily financial transactions.

Assignments 2

1. Write in your diary (in not more than 300 words) about a small event of your life that left an abiding impact on you.
2. Write a story that you heard from your mother/grandmother when you were a small child.
3. Birbal was a man of wit, famous for his quick and wise answers, solutions to most intricate problems as well as his acute sense of humor. There have been some other wise men like him. Have you heard of any such wise man? Write a story from his life that proves his wit and sense of humour.

Chapter 3

Connect to the Source

I am 'A' among all the letters.
– Lord Krishna, Geeta, 10:33

To truly know is to know that: all knowledge starts from a divine source. Thus, the right beginning in any sphere of knowledge – and writing is not an exception – is to seek a beginning in the source of all beginnings.

In a park, once a man was playing with some children. A huge rock laid in the middle of the park posing a threat to everyone and it needed to be removed. The man encouraged the children to remove the rock if they could. They were three children but the rock was heavy and big. They used sticks and their muscles but the rock did not budge a bit.

"*Tired are we*", gasped the children, "*we tried our best but the rock is not moving*".

The man asked, "*Did you really try everything?*"

"*Yes, we did*", the children panted.

The man said: "*You did not try one thing!*"

"*What?*" – asked they.

"*You did not approach me for help*".

And now the three children, with the additional help of the man, succeeded in removing the rock.

When we make an attempt and fail, perhaps we did not try one thing – we did not ask God for help! God is not present only in temples and mosques, churches and synagogues for periodic worship. He lives in us ... with us ... for us ... every moment and for everything.

The Lord is the Law...

The same law applies to writing as it applies to all other businesses of life. Whenever we 'connect' to the source of all knowledge and wisdom, we succeed in bringing out the best pearls from the deep oceans of our mind and heart.

There is no need to necessarily name this 'source' as God. As Shakespeare said: *"What's in a name? That which we call a rose, by any other name would smell as sweet."* The 'Lord' and the 'law' is the same thing. If we call a chair a 'chair', it allows us to sit in it; if we call a chair something else, still it will allow us to sit in it.

The vital truth is that there is a greater me in me, a deeper and subtler mind beyond my superficial thought pattern. Whatever that power is, whatever name can be given to that hidden entity, it is true that we find our best guidance from our 'inner' self. That inner self gives us in proportion to our faith. If you trust, it will give; if not, it won't – and this is the immutable law.

Our mind as a computer...

The question is: How can we connect to that source? How does it work? The answer is, through our subconscious mind. God or that greater self will not appear before us in the human form to guide us on our way. That power is all-pervading, all knowing and we are both its centre and its medium. Take the example of a computer with a powerful network or the Internet. Suppose we want to empower our computer system with a new and useful program. This program will enable the computer to work faster and with greater efficiency. What do we do? There is no other way than to use the computer itself to download that useful program from the Internet or install it through a CD using its own CD-drive. The computer itself became the medium of the 'installation' as well as its beneficiary. In the same way, the Divine works through us for us.

Our mind is a live computer. It has a conscious centre, same as the Arithmetic Logic Unit (ALU) of a normal computer. It also has a subconscious centre which can be compared to a remote Internet site. The subconscious centre of the mind is connected to an inexhaustible 'Server' – the Super Conscious -- which has all information on all topics. It has fathomless knowledge and infallible guidance on all aspects of life and for everyone. It makes no difference if you are a child and want to have some novel information on a cow or a chimpanzee, or you are a versatile genius who is doing research on the pre-historic age. The Super Conscious has all that you need for your level.

How do we do it practically?

Whenever you have to write on a topic, and you need better guidance, just calm your mind and say silently, with faith: "*I am connected to my Greater Self. I know how to write on this topic. The required knowledge is coming to me*". Say it honestly, calmly and patiently ... not in a hurried state, not with doubt, not with an intention to give it a 'try' .... and then relax! Based on the urgency of your question and firmness of your faith, an answer will '*pop-up*' in due course. The answer will '*dawn*' in your heart as a '*silent whisper*' or a '*flashing light of idea*' after which you will know that you '*know*' and your curiosity is fulfilled.

The subconscious mind can give you every detail from the beginning to end, as to how to write on the given topic. Or it may just give you an idea to consult certain books, people, resources, etc., and there you will surely find the necessary help. It is also possible that your subconscious mind will give you only a glimmer of the first line of your article or, may be, only its title. Whatever it is, the subconscious mind knows that you can 'follow the clue' and proceed further. Trust in its wisdom and act upon its guidance, immediately, believing that once you start, the remaining help will also follow.

Once you have submitted a request to your subconscious mind and have added the necessary faith, be ready to receive the answer. A person, who believes that the power of his prayer will bring in rains, carries an umbrella with him. Otherwise, he has no trust in his prayer and the universe does never help people who do not trust. If you believe (and you must!) that the invisible power will inspire you with the necessary details for your writing, follow these four basic steps:

The Four Basic Steps to follow the subconscious guidance...

1. **Always carry a small note-book** and a pen or pencil with you. The subconscious power may respond to your query anywhere suddenly, while you are walking or traveling, shopping or just sitting peacefully in a park. As soon as the idea 'pops-up', note it down <u>immediately</u> since, like dreams, sudden ideas soon tend to slip away from our memory. Moreover, an inspiration usually does not come twice. It may flash anywhere suddenly like a lightning and if you cannot 'capture' it fast, it's gone forever. Don't wait for

the details. If it is just a title that has occured to you, note it down. Later, when you are at home, transfer this idea fairly and cleanly written in a beautiful diary you can name as MY BOOK OF IDEAS. I have been using this method since long. Even this book you are reading is a product of a sudden thought which I noted down in my Book of Ideas to work on later.

In other words, whenever you have an inspired thought, initial lines for a poem, title of a book or a novel, points for an essay or article, conclusions for a research, questions for an important survey, headings for a report, hints for a discovery, or anything on this earth, immediately note it down in your small portable notebook and then transfer it to your Book of Ideas. Leave enough space (suppose one full page) in the idea book so that later, when more thoughts are gravitated on that particular subject, you can put it down on the relevant page. You will wonder how things clarified by and by and you will be able to write even a full book.

While this process is very useful for aspiring writers, it is equally beneficial for students and amateurs who have smaller projects like: writing an annual report for the office or the department, school project or assignment on a certain topic, an inspiring talk or a lecture, newspaper reports or articles, radio talk, and so on.

2. **Act fast.** The word <u>immediately</u> has been underlined in the above paragraph to draw your attention. For reasons not properly known to human minds, the Universal Mind working through you loves speed and torrent. When ideas flow, they flow suddenly and some times in such volumes that will leave you amazed.

Your responsibility, then, is to act quickly and note down as much details as you can. Don't worry as to how you will be able to manage them later, coordinate all the information and incorporate all the points. Leave the details on that *Great Supplier of the Ideas*. If you have ever observed, the universe always has more than necessary, contrary to our popular belief that resources are dwindling away. The grass could be less green but it is richly green. On trees, there could be fewer leaves and on deserts lesser sands but that's not the case. In an apple, there are seeds more than necessary. In oceans there is water more than we need. Nature reflects the infinite wealth of the Almighty and everything in surplus. It does not mean, however, that we should be careless and neglect our natural resources. Remember, it is the same nature that fills trees with more than necessary leaves, does not waste even a single leaf. Each leaf that falls on the ground, adds to the property of the soil and is re-used and recycled in nature's own way.

The same profusion is expressed in the world of ideas. So worry not if some points are left, if some streams of thought are missed out. Still you have more than necessary to start on. Your role is just to 'hold' the ideas immediately as they flood in. You have to be ready and attentive on your part.

3. **Say grateful words.** Whenever a valuable idea has occured to you, it is very important to say a generous "Thank You" to the Universal Mind. For example, say: "O God! (or O the Universal Mind!) Thank you so much for this great idea. I am sure you will supply me with more ideas to accomplish my work". When you say these words, mean it. Be grateful from your heart. In fact, the Universal Mind does not need or depend upon your 'thanks', you yourself need it. A mind smoothened by the kind feelings of gratefulness becomes a humble ground for receiving more and more ideas. Don't think that only human beings need thank you's and only they can understand its value. When we go into the deeper worlds of existence and look into things either with a scientific or a spiritual perspective, we come to realize that even such things as are labeled 'inanimate' or lifeless by us, do have life. Each atom, each cell is alive, vibrating with consciousness and understands the language and feelings of love and gratitude.

4. **Start Writing.** Make a tentative plan and an outline of your project and start writing. Do not wait for acquisition of 'complete information' before you start writing on any subject. Start with an initial understanding and as you will go forward, thoughts will react with thoughts, ideas will blend into ideas, imagination will pull more stuff and you will be able to complete your work, if you just keep on writing. May be your writing will not be too good, too praiseworthy, but remember you are just a beginner. Perfection will come in time.

For the time being, just follow these four rules and you will see how you will achieve wonderful results.

Using intuition...

Have heard about mathematicians or chess-players who even defeated computers though a computer can calculate a hundred times faster than a man? You might also have heard about people who were sitting a thousand miles away from their close friend or relative and knew, without any physical means of communication, exactly what happened with that friend or relative.

Many accidents have been prevented with the use of intuition or telepathic knowledge, many discoveries have been made. You have yourself experienced many such moments in life when you 'guessed' something and your guess was right. You expected to meet an old friend, with no apparent hope to meet him or her, and you met. The postman knocked at the door and your 'sixth sense' told you whose letter it may be. The phone rang and you knew who was on the other end. In fact, when you were a child you had a plenty of intuitive knowledge, but as you grew up, your 'logical' mind suppressed your 'intuitive' mind and all the charm was lost.

Intuition is nature's radar system. She has equipped every living creature with this enormously powerful system for the purpose of their survival and, also, to help them gain insight beyond time and space. Using this powerful radar, the bats, though they are near-blind, fly so fast in the night without hitting the walls, and find their victims with their inherent power of 'echolocation'. Using this natural system, some birds and animals can predict a storm, an earthquake, or weather conditions. Using this device that works beyond the realms of logic, hearts unite in this world in a loving manner and some people distract us even though they have apparently done no harm to us.

As *"faith is the evidence of things not seen"* (The Bible, Hebrews 11:1 (NKJV), intuition is also a powerful system that always gives you the right information beyond the limits of your physical senses and devices. But we need to depend on it and trust in our "pure hunches". Here "pure hunches" means your mind should be free from doubts and prejudices, in complete faith, and devoid of any ill, negative feelings.

The three important tools to develop intuitive skills...

Such an intuitive skill can practically be developed by using three simple tools:

- Daily meditation

- Practice of inner silence
- Creative anticipation

Meditation is something well known to all, but perhaps people fail to understand its significance in developing our writing skills. When we meditate, we sit silently in a comfortable posture for a feasible period (10-15 minutes), still the activities of our mind and concentrate on something. <u>Meditation is usually of two types</u>: Active Meditation and Passive Meditation. Active meditation is when we concentrate on an object of our choice. Passive Meditation is when we concentrate on nothing but let our mind flow through a train of thoughts.

For a beginner, passive meditation is easier and can facilitate active meditation later on. For this, just sit relaxed, undisturbed, calm, and peaceful. Breathe easily but a bit deeply, close your eyes. Now see what your mind sees. Be an observer. Judge nothing. Don't think what is right or wrong, moral or immoral, logical or illogical, true or false. May be your mind will show you a killing scene. Neither be afraid nor cynical, watch it. May be your mind will think something abominable and heinous, let it. May be your mind will visualize something too impossible like a winged horse, but let it.

Passive meditation opens up the hidden vistas of the mind whereby more intuitions can peek through. That's because we let our mind loose, unfasten the bridles of logics and judgmental views. As such, we are able to receive 'unfiltered guidance from unseen horizons of sub-consciousness.'

After 10-15 days, switch to active meditation. For this also, sit relaxed, undisturbed, calm, and peaceful. Breathe easily but a bit deeply, close your eyes. Now focus on a certain object, just as a flower. You can also focus on a writing project you have been given, e.g., "*Global Warming Vs Global Warning*". Think deeply on this topic, let every related picture (mountain, icebergs, plains, rivers, trees, the earth, the oceans, etc.) appear in your mind; let every contextual thought flow. Don't deviate from this topic for, say, 10-15 minutes. In the end, you will come out with quite a clear picture that how to start the write-up, what to put in the body text and how to end or conclude the subject. However, it takes practice and you will get frequent successes later on as you keep on practicing.

<u>Practice of inner silence</u> is also important and is dealt separately in one of the next chapters.

Creative anticipation is perhaps the most useful and direct mechanism for tapping our intuitive skills. Practically, it means depending more and more on imagination than on reasoning. Reasoning is a faculty of conscious mind and is based on material evidence. For example: "*My English teacher is a very angry lady. She always scolds. She will scold me today because I was absent yesterday*". This is conscious or inductive reasoning based on the fact that the English teacher is usually a strict lady. Inductive reasoning is always based on "past experiences or facts" and cannot see anything beyond these cycles of previous causes and conditions. But we know that all new causes and conditions come out of thought or supposition that is unconditional and deductive in nature. For example, men had never flown in air before the airplane was 'anticipated' in some minds. All new inventions and discoveries happen out of "creative anticipation", free from the worries of contrary evidences of the past, depending on no previous existing conditions. Realities are shaped in the realms of the mind.

So .... should we not reason? Is reasoning bad or useless? Are all decisions of life taken 'imaginatively', without the use of logic? The answer is: Reasoning is a very wonderful thing and a power that is bestowed upon mankind only. As it is said earlier, it is a faculty of the conscious mind, and our conscious mind is there because we can consciously decide what to do and what not to. Therefore, all general decisions in life depend on conscious reasoning. What to eat, what to wear, which vocation to adopt, in which city to live, which service to join .... there are hundreds of examples of our daily concerns that relate to our conscious judgment. However, many subtler questions of life are often dealt with the use of a "deeper mind" that thinks beyond reasons. When it becomes difficult for us to decide what to do and what not to, it is useful to tap the power of intuition.

<u>Creative anticipation</u> means intentionally using imagination to get the positive, desired result. Instead of thinking in a conventional way, we think differently. For example, "*All say my English teacher is a very strict lady but I know she is calm and loving. I am regular to school but yesterday I had some problem. I am sure she won't scold me*".

The use of your creative anticipation will develop your power of intuition, because thoughts driven by faith, positive expectancy and purity of intention lead to spiritually uplifted conditions. When you expect good and great, you receive good and great. Your anticipation may be wrong in the beginning for a number of times but then things will start taking shape as you would want.

Some practical hints for "Creative Anticipation"...

- Next month is your birthday. Make a list of your close friends and relatives and the gifts you expect from each of them. Later compare the list with the actual gifts you received from each of them.
- A new staff member is going to join your office/department in a couple of days. Anticipate his/her personality and write down the details. Match these details after that person joined your team.
- Ask one of your friends to write a 'message' for you on a piece of paper, fold it and give it to you. Guess beforehand what the message is.
- Guess your boss' mood tomorrow in the office.
- Guess what the weather is going to be like next Sunday.
- What lunch your colleague has brought today?
- One of your classmates/co-workers is absent today. Guess the reason of his/her absence and confirm it later.
- Next time when your mobile rings, close your eyes and guess promptly who might be calling.
- Ask your brother or sister or friend to collect some tit-bits from the household (such as pins, clips, spoon, chocolate, needle, and many common items easily found in any house). Let him/her put these items (not more than 10) in a tray and cover the tray without showing you any item. Now do your guesswork and list the items as per your intuition. Match to see how correct you are. Next time, the items should be somewhat changed.

There are many such practices that you can think of on your own. The more you use them, the more you benefit. <u>Just remember: there's difference between an intuition and a random thought.</u> When an intuition comes you can identify it by its firmness, speed, definiteness, its convincing manner, its doubtless nature. So, go on and tap the miraculous power of the mind to become a powerful writer.

Ten Top Tips

1. When we make every attempt and fail, perhaps we did not try one thing – we didn't ask God for help!
2. Whenever we connect to the 'source' of all knowledge and wisdom, we succeed in bringing out the best.
3. The great source of all knowledge and wisdom acts through our subconscious mind.
4. Our mind is like a computer equipped with the Internet.
5. The subconscious mind can give you every detail – from beginning to end – on any given topic.
6. Faith is essential if we would like to receive guidance.
7. We should immediately note down any valuable idea that comes to our mind.
8. We should act fast on that idea and start writing with whatever initial knowledge we have.
9. Intuition is nature's radar system that helps us to gain insight beyond time and space.
10. The power of intuition can be developed by meditation, practice of inner silence and creative anticipation.

Exercise 3

Match your answers with those given on the ANSWER PAGE. Give yourself 2 marks for each correct answer.

1. **What was the one thing the children hadn't tried?**
   - A. Using their boots
   - B. Using stronger sticks
   - C. Asking the man's help
   - D. Praying to God

2. **Who said: "What's in a name? That which we call a rose, by any other name would smell as sweet." ?**
   - A. William Shakespeare
   - B. John Milton
   - C. William Wordsworth
   - D. Anonymous

3. **What is the secret of a powerful writing?**
   - A. It is complex and wordy
   - B. It is inspired from our 'inner' self
   - C. It is highly logical and occult
   - D. It is superficial

4. **How does the Greater Mind provide us with ideas for writing?**
   - A. Through our subconscious mind
   - B. Through a computer system
   - C. Through the Internet
   - D. Through our teachers

5. **What is the most essential quality if we would like our subconscious mind to help us with creative ideas?**
   - A. Doubt
   - B. Fear
   - C. Care
   - D. Faith

6. **In this chapter, the terms 'dawn', 'silent whisper', and 'flashing light' are used to describe:**
   - A. How the subconscious mind reacts adversely to our request
   - B. How the invisible power helps us to find a resource
   - C. When definite ideas are instinctively given to us in response
   - D. When we don't know what to do and what not to

Assignments 3

1. Based on the statements given below, identify those great men who believed in their dreams and achieved them. Choose names from the list provided in the box below. (***Check answers on the ANSWER PAGE***)

A. We dreamt of making the most comprehensive 'search engine' in the world by linking together a number of websites and in 1996, we set up Google.

B. I was partially blind and deaf. They said I was useless, but I studied the behaviour of ants and other creatures and came out with a new discipline in science – i.e., sociobiology.

C. I gave a new direction to Mathematics by proving that all "invariants" could be expressed in terms of a finite number. In 1900, during the Second International Congress of Mathematicians in Paris, I presented my famous speech entitled "The Problems of Mathematics".

D. I took no sword in my hands and, with the might of my will-power and high morale, I freed my country from the most powerful rulers of the world.

E. I was born in a wealthy noble family in Russia. I could spend my life in luxury but I chose to live like a saint and help the poor peasants.

F. I was one of the prominent founders of Western Philosophy. They gave me poison for my new thoughts and moral teachings but I believed in what I said and died for my belief.

G. I claimed that the earth turns on its axis, gave the scientific reason of eclipses and many revolutionary theories of mathematics and astronomy.

H. We believed that an invention should not only fill the need of the time but it must also be efficient and economical. With this view, we founded a world class company of high quality computers and accessories.

I. I wrote the famous book – "The Republic" and described the nature and qualities of an ideal state much before modern political system had evolved.

J. I failed a thousand times and yet believed in my dreams. I made hundreds of useful inventions including the electric bulb.

> Thomas Edison, Larry Page and Sergey Brin, Aryabhata, Tolostoy, Mahatma Gandhi, Plato, William Hewlett and David Packard, David Hilbert, A.O. Wilson, Socrates

2. Who said this? (*Check answers on the ANSWER PAGE*)

   (A) One of the striking differences between a cat and a lie is that a cat has only nine lives.
   (B) There are two forces: fate and human effort - All men depend on and are bound by these, there is nothing else.
   (C) I often quote myself. It adds spice to my conversation.
   (D) Short is my date, but deathless my renown.
   (E) To be, or not to be: that is the question.

   > William Shakespeare (Hamlet), George Bernard Shaw, Mark Twain, Maharshi Vyas (The Mahabharata), Homer (The Iliad).

Chapter 4

How Some Great Books were Written

Writing a novel is like driving a car at night. You can see only as far as your headlights but you can make the whole trip that way.

– E.L. Doctorow

There is no great writer in this world who did not tap his subconscious faculty in writing. The truth is, the more a writer is dependent on his or her intuitive wisdom, greater the work he or she brings out to the world. The simple reason is that everything that is sublime and great, superb and spontaneous comes from the realm other than our limited wisdom can understand.

The 'fools' (!) who ruled literature...

The 'un-classic' writer of timeless classics

William Shakespeare was not a very educated and well versed writer. He did not even study much about his contemporary writers and perhaps this was the reason his writing was unique, bearing no influence of others. Many people doubted that he did not write all those great dramas since how could such a simple and un-scholarly person write such timeless classics? However, such foolish doubts are not entertained by lovers of Shakespeare and his greatness cannot be challenged.

The 'self-sabotaging' poet

The great Sanskrit poet, **Kalidasa**, who is often referred to as "*The Shakespeare of India*", wrote such marvelous books like '**Abhigyan Shakuntalam**' – so superb a classic that Goethe (the great German poet) is believed to have said after reading its German translation that this book reflects the beauty of heaven on earth. However Kalidasa was a simpleton. He was so foolish that it was said that once he was cutting the same branch of the tree on which he was sitting. Who could believe that the same geek would become a renowned poet one day?

The 'robber' turned to be a kind poet

The wonderful epic of the '*Ramayana*' is today translated into almost all major languages of the world. It is a piece of evergreen world literature with its lofty ideals and divine elements as well as the unsurpassable beauty enshrined in its diction and story. Today there are many editions and versions, but the original 'Ramayana' was written by **Valmiki**. He was, in fact, a merciless robber and killer but later he became detached from the worldly desires and spent the rest of his life praying and meditating as a recluse. Once, while he was in his meditation in a lonely jungle, he heard the pensive cry of a bird. A hunter had shot an arrow hitting one of the birds in their moments of love. The pitiful cry of the bird rent Valmiki's heart. He opened his eyes moved by the deep-felt grief of the dying bird and suddenly a verse flowed from his mouth. It was his curse for the careless shooter and meant something like this:

> *"O the Killer of the bird in moments of loving unity*
> *May you find no peace till the times of eternity!"*

As he said these words, he was amazed at his own creativity. These were beautiful poetic lines nobody had ever said them before. Thus, poetry was born spontaneously from Valmiki. This was the first poem and Valmiki became the 'first poet'.

It all starts from the heart...

What all these examples imply for is that great writings arise from the depth of one's heart, through the process of inspiration, and not from knowledge and witchcraft of words. One may be a versed grammarian, a person with thousands of words at his control, he might have read volumes of books to sharpen his knowledge, oceans of information might be surging in his mind but writing will flow only when he will tap the potentials of his inner vision, his intuitive powers, to utilize all the knowledge and information he has.

This is not to say that writing is a fool's job for which no knowledge is required. It will be ridiculous to conclude that one can be an eminent writer with poor resources of vocabulary and no knowledge of grammar and other disciplines. It simply means that once a person has an 'urge' for writing, he need not wait to gain knowledge, to learn grammar and cram all the words of the dictionary. He must start from the pitch of his heart, believing that every necessary thing will follow. When an 'idea' is born, it starts finding its expressions, channels and means. Idea is important, desire is essential; a genuine interest is the prime requisite. Start with these properties and one day you will become a great writer. Note: I did not say that you will become a Longfellow or Victor Hugo, Tolstoy or Maupassant overnight. They were *they*, you are *you*. They could not be like you nor can you be like them. Writing is that vast and immense ocean where everyone who steps into it creates a new island. Here everyone is a Columbus and a Vasco D' Gama, provided he believes in himself and sets his sail to explore the infinite worlds surging inside him.

Experience teaches wisdom...

Experience teaches wisdom. Knowledge comes through practice. You cannot hope to be a perfect writer in the very beginning, but gradually refinement will come. It is like swimming. If someone tells you "*I will go into water after I've learnt swimming*", won't you laugh at him? Without going into water nobody can learn swimming. In the beginning, the swimmer has to face difficulties. He cannot swim longer and farther. He's soon gets tired. His breathing becomes short. He cannot dive for long. He has no clear knowledge about the right movements, about relaxation techniques. Sometimes he intakes water in his lungs. But, gradually, one day he becomes an expert swimmer who can cross the English Channel, who can daunt the mighty waves of the ocean.

Writing is learnt by writing. There is no other shortcut. Everyone is capable of writing because everyone is capable of thinking. Writing is nothing but putting our thoughts in black and white. There is no human being whose heart is not filled with an expression, whose mind is not imbued with some thought. The only difference is that most people don't believe or care that they can write. Those who believe they can, they strive and become writers and people with excellent penmanship.

Don't care what others say...

The most important thing is that you must rely on your inner power to write, and the other things will follow. Haven't you seen a child who hasn't yet learnt to speak? He strives his best to use his facial expressions, manipulate his gestures and signs, stretch every nerve, make all possible movements to express something he wants to. And people follow. Nobody complains that the child's gestures are unclear. The intensity counts. Be like that child, start expressing.

No writer can please everyone. You cannot always have people who praise you. Even **Bhavabhuti**, a noted Sanskrit poet, had to feel the gloom of neglect and say *"perhaps someone like me will appreciate my feelings one day"* (Utpastsyate cha mam kopi samandharma).

When I was 10-11 years old, I had started composing poems. Well, nobody can expect from a child of that age to be a veteran poet but my mother always had a word of praise for me. She even showed my poems to two of my uncles – one was a pessimist and cynic, the other was an optimist and enthusiast. After reading my poems, the former commented: *"O God! No proper rhyming, no meters observed. What these poems are!"* And it left a bad taste in my mouth. I felt I should give up all this. The latter said: *"Great for his age! I would have liked to publish them in a magazine, but there is time for that. He should focus more on solidifying his thoughts"*. "Solidifying his thoughts" was not something which came as clear to me at that age but I was happy. I knew he liked my poems and encouraged me. I kept on going. I did not know meters; I did not know those erudite rules of prosody. I think even today I don't know ... but I know I can write.

Rely on the unseen...

Relying on the power of the unseen, the great Greek poet **Homer** wrote *Iliad* and *Odyssey*. Though he was blind, the tales of the Trojan War which he depicted, the minuteness of human character which he portrayed, have made him immortal.

In 1990, when **J.K. Rowling** was traveling in a train from Manchester to London, it was the same power that inspired this divorced and struggling poor woman to write the Harry Potter series. She responded to the call and became a millionaire whose wealth almost equals to that of the Queen of England.

It was the same power that charged the heart and mind of a small girl, **Anne Frank**, who was captured by the Nazi terrorists in 1942 and was murdered in 1945 among millions of the Jewish victims of the Holocaust. At that time she was as young as 15 years. She depicted the atrocious conditions of her imprisonment in a diary which was published in 1947 as ***The Diary of a Young Girl*** and became a well known book, a classic masterpiece that portrayed the cruel traits of fascism from a child's perspective.

How a scientist - Dr. Jekyll - changed himself into a criminal - Mr. Hyde - by taking a medicinal powder, was the stupendous theme of a suspense story that has been casting its spell over readers since 1886. When ***Robert Louis Stevenson*** wrote this world-famous novel - ***The Strange Case of Dr Jekyll and Mr Hyde*** – the idea came to him from the super conscious entity in the form of a dream.

Stephanie Meyer trusted this divine and unseen when she dreamt of a beautiful girl and a disguised vampire who was lustful for the smell of her blood. The book that she wrote – Twilight – became a successful book as well as a movie sensation.

The idea of ***Frankenstein*** sparked in ***Mary Shelley's*** mind, when she was only 18, as she utterly wanted an inspiration for a ghost-story and then saw a peculiar dream of a doctor who collects different parts of a body and infuses life into a deadly creature. This bone-shaking terror did not only prove to be a renowned book but also a mind-wobbling film.

The successful plot of ***Misery*** – that tells the tale of a horrendous lady who captivates and kills a writer and binds the poor writer's novel in his own dead skin -- was handed over to ***Stephen King*** during a dream while he was sleeping in his plane.

And far beyond all these human examples, realize the potency of great scriptures of the world that were divinely revealed through the Messengers of God. Even if the whole humanity combine their best efforts, if the most renowned writers of the world form a mighty association to work together, none can produce another ***Quran*** or the ***Bible***, or the ***Geeta***, or the ***Hidden Words***. What can be a greater proof of the fact that great writings are always inspired by the Great Mind?

Authority and greatness comes from on high...

Have you ever watched a traffic police? He is not a special person. He has no powerful muscles nor is he wealthy or a scholar of some kind. He has no weapons in his hands but perhaps a small baton, and a whistle that he blows. And yet when he blows his whistle, the richest and the most mightiest people of the city bring their cars to a halt.

Another example is of a surgeon. He will take the patient, a much loved person in your life, inside the operation theatre, and operate on him. Inspite of knowing all this, you still trust the doctor and let him take charge of your beloved person happily.

What gives authority to a simple traffic constable that even the mightiest of people stop at his behest? What makes a surgeon so reliable that even though he has all the devices to kill, he is counted upon as a giver of life? This is the authority of Law, the authority of Knowledge. A traffic constable is backed up by the law. A doctor is trusted because he wields the power and faith of his acquired knowledge.

The messengers of God also appear in human forms. None of them were different from us. Yet all what these messengers revealed were the words of God. What they said, carried the might and approval of the Almighty, authority of the all-powerful. Therefore, even though centuries have passed and though human intellect has surpassed the limited boundaries of the past ages, the truth and wisdom contained in the aforesaid Holy Scriptures stand irrefutable.

Likewise, when we follow the guidance of the super conscious, rely on our instincts and guts, believe in the inner voice prompting us to write something, tap our subconscious mind and trust our pure intuitions, whatever comes out from our heart is divinely charged. Whatever we write becomes superhuman and delectable. On the contrary, if we just rely on our limited wisdom, the produce is sure to be of inferior quality.

Believe in yourself and trust the songs, the music, and the feelings that overflow in your inner heart. Care for no comments if they are not meant to boost your morale. Just rely on the unseen and go on. As the quotation in the beginning of this chapter clarifies, more mysterious things will unfold as you go along and you will wonder what you wrote! This journey has a hesitant beginning but a romantic end. Know it to be a truth that every sincere writer does only one thing – grab the pen in his hand – and the rest is done by some other power.

Ten Top Tips

1. The more a writer is dependent on his or her intuitive wisdom, greater the work he or she brings out in the world.
2. Great writings came from the depth of one's heart, through a process of inner inspiration.
3. Once we have an 'urge' for writing, other necessary things will automatically follow.
4. An idea is more important than grammatical knowledge and word power.
5. One cannot hope to be a perfect writer at the outset, but gradually refinement will come.
6. No writer can please everyone. You cannot always have people who praise you.
7. Great writings are always inspired by the great mind.
8. We must not care about negative and disheartening comments from people for our sincere writings.
9. Writing is a journey with a hesitant beginning but a romantic end.
10. Every sincere writer does only one thing – to grab the pen in his hand – and the rest is done by some other power.

Exercise 4

Match your answers with those given on the ANSWER PAGE. Give yourself 2 marks for each correct answer.

1. What is <u>TRUE</u> about William Shakespeare?
   - A. He was highly educated.
   - B. He had a deep study of his contemporary writers.
   - C. None of his books were written by himself.
   - D. He wrote great books of all times.

2. Which book, according to the German poet, Goethe, reflects the beauty of heaven on earth?
   - A. The Ramayana
   - B. War and Peace
   - C. Abhigyan Shakuntalam
   - D. Arabian Nights

3. What is the most important thing for a writer?
   - A. Knowledge of grammar
   - B. Idea
   - C. Vocabulary
   - C. Style

4. Which statement is TRUE?
   - A. Writing is a fool's job for which no knowledge is required.
   - B. One can be an eminent writer with poor word-power.
   - C. One must start from his heart, believing that other necessary thing will follow.
   - D. One must learn grammar and cram all the words of the dictionary before one starts to write.

5. Who wrote The Diary of a Young Girl?
   - A. Anne Frank
   - B. R. L. Stevenson
   - C. J.K. Rowling
   - D. Adolf Hitler

6. Whatever we write becomes superhuman and delectable – when?
   - A. When we write something after a great research.
   - B. When we quote many references from different authors.
   - C. When we write after a lot of study.
   - D. When we follow the guidance of the super conscious.

Assignments 4

1. Write a short biography (between 250-300 words) on any two of the following writers/poets: (Model answer given on ANSWER PAGE)

    Milton, W.B. Yeats, Agatha Christie, Dostoyevsky.

2. Match the books with their writers. Write the corresponding letter from the list given below. (***Check answers on the ANSWER PAGE***)

    Note: All titles are taken from this book only.

    1) Alice in the Wonderland   ____
    2) Gulliver's Travels   ____
    3) Leaves of Grass   ____
    4) The Ramayana   ____
    5) A Clockwork Orange   ____
    6) Odyssey   ____
    7) Divan   ____
    8) The Divine Comedy   ____
    9) Harry Potter   ____
    10) Devdas   ____
    11) David Copperfield   ____
    12) The Diary of a Young Girl   ____
    13) Misery   ____
    14) The Strange Case of Dr. Jekyll and Mr. Hyde   ____
    15) Frankenstein   ____

    (A) Hafez   (B) Mary Shelley   (C) Homer
    (D) Sharat Chandra Chattopadhyay   (E) Anthony Burgess
    (F) J.K. Rowling   (G) Dante Alighieri   (H) R. L. Stevenson
    (I) Valmiki   (J) Charles Dickens   (K) Anne Frank
    (L) Lewis Carroll (M) Jonathan Swift   (N) Stephen King
    (O) Walt Whitman

Chapter 5

Observe and Imagine

To imagine yourself inside another person is what a story writer does in every piece of work. It is his first step and his last step too, I suppose.

– Eudora Weltu

Some splendid people can never be forgotten, like Kishore Massab (we as children used to call him). This poor youth, a trainee teacher, was picked up by my uncle who was a headmaster and brought home one evening to be 'imposed' upon me as my home tutor. I was hardly 8 or 9 years. I looked at this 'handsome tyrant' with great awe! He was hardly 18 years old, fair-complexioned, wearing a traditional *dhoti-kurta* like a typical Indian *'guruji'*, and maneuvering a sobriety on his face which crisscrossed his handsome and innocent looks. And now he was sharing my room, taking breakfast and lunch with me, strolling with me in our barn-house after evening meals, and waking me up in the morning to join him for Yoga.

Before anything else, I must tell you something very interesting about Kishore Massab. In one of his emotional moments while teaching us (my cousins and many neighboring children soon joined our lantern-side evening classes), he once declared very emphatically: *"Know ye all, which three things I would never do in my life?"*

"What"? We children inquired.

"Firstly I will never marry. Secondly, I will never wear that ugly pantaloon and shirt type of dress and, thirdly, I will never chew betel leaves", said Kishore Massab. For those who don't know, betel leaves or *'paan'* are typical Indian mouth-fresheners chewed with lime, catechu, nuts and tobacco-made flavors, etc.

We were so very proud of our Kishore Massab.

Years passed by. Kishore Massab became a government teacher and left our home. I settled in town and graduated from university. Then, once I visited my village after years. One day, some guests were inside when I had just come from a walk and was sitting on the verandah. My aunt called: *"Come in, won't like to see a very important person of your life?"* I went in. It was a great surprise to see Kishore Massab after years. He was not in his typical *dhoti-kurta*, but in a suit, the redness of 'paan' coloured his lips and he had come with his wife.

The moon-lit night in the village...

It was shocking for me at that time but life is like that ... unpredictable. In terms of writing the same holds true. It seems to be promising something at the beginning and those promises are not fake, but then there is an unseen destiny that leads us to something else.

But that's not the end of Kishore Massab. What I basically wanted to say was his emphasis on brushing up imagination skills. After our supper, Kishore Massab used to take me for a stroll at our farm-house. It was a natural scenic spot, with bundles of corns heaped up in the barn, wheat plants waving their green frocks far away, cows licking their lovely calves and, above all, the full moon of a typical night shedding its splendours over a smiling little world of our pretty sweet village. But I was a child, perhaps too young to appreciate this beauty of Nature and was rather keen to go to bed. But Kishore Massab won't leave my hands and would say: "*Well, do you see that lovely moon? Say a few words on her.*" I had no escape than to observe the moon and finally come up with a couple of sentences like: "*the moon is yellow ... it is bright and beautiful*". Next night I had to observe the beauty and the silence of night and say something. Next to next night it rained, frogs croaked and Kishore Massab had a new topic. "Say something" was an everlasting story and there was no escape from this task.

That time I may have liked it or not, but today I know that Kishore Massab planted a seed of 'Observe and Imagine' in my tender heart. I salute him today for this gift that he had silently placed in my inner being. People who really care that his or her children should grow up to capable writers – and by writers I don't mean Shakespeares and Miltons but anyone who is well expressive of his ideas – must follow the example of Kishore Massab.

Everything tells something about itself...

Observation and imagination are twins or, say, two aspects of the same coin. Without observation, imagination cannot develop and without imagination observation is but a dumb onlooker, a flightless bird.

Everything tells something about itself, if we can observe and listen. Every soul has something to say, every atom has a marvelous story, every inanimate stone has but a momentous message, only if we are imaginative.

Try to penetrate everything, go deeper into its meaning, read between the lines, imagine the scenario which is not apparent but hidden. Once you step into this world of imagination, layer by layer every truth will reveal and you will have enough stuff to write a whole book, much less to talk of small articles and write-ups. For example, you might have read in yesterday's newspaper a tiny piece of news in an unnoticeable corner of the page – "Three Peacocks found dead in the City Zoo". Stop here and focus on the 'inside stories' using your own imagination. How could the peacocks die? Are the zoo officials taking proper care of the endangered birds? There could be some smuggling of peacock feathers, they are so beautiful and used for several luxurious adornments. Are a gang of smugglers rampant in the town? What are the police doing? Corruption? Or have the peacocks died due to food poisoning? What contaminant prevailed in the foods supplied by the vendors to the zoo? All are dying for money only! No one cares ... no responsibility! Or have the deaths of the peacocks resulted from excessive heat? Global warming! Several birds and animals are extinct just due to climatic changes!

You saw how... one simple news can suggest so many aspects of a thing that is not even reported in the news. Expand these ideas and pen them down ... preferably on a daily or weekly basis. This will not only enhance your writing skill but also your personality by enriching your insight and susceptibilities.

A couple of sparrows building their nest, a bee humming over a luscious flower, a poor child boot-polishing in the street, a homeless girl on a railway platform, a smiling policeman, a roaring school master, a skyscraper, a whistling train, the aura of a colorful morning – observe and imagine – they've to tell you many stories.

Imagination lets you develop rapport with your reader...

The tool of imagination does not only help you to sharpen your insight and fathom into the depths of every object or situation, it also enables you to develop a keen rapport with your reader.

Often, the main objective of your writing will be to communicate something to a potential reader or a group of readers. While writing, keep that potential reader in your view. It will help you orient your writing in such a way so as to grab the attention of that reader. You will be able to choose the right words, phrases and syntaxes that correspond to the level and aptitude of that reader.

For example, if you are writing a script for children, imagine those children in your mind. Where are these children, which country, which geographical location, which cultural background, what age-group, level of education, rich or poor, modern or rural? Once these imaginations are clear, you will be self-guided to use short and brisk sentences, lively and imaginative accounts, playful and humorous ambience, etc.

On the other hand, suppose, you are writing a research paper to be read over to a glitterati of scientists in a scholastic seminar. Imagine these scientists; see them clearly wearing their high-power specks (!), loading a grave dignity on their eye-brows, ready to listen to no jokes but all facts, illustrated in their knowledge, confirmed in their convictions! Keeping them in view, you will be able to tailor your writing along a high profile, authentic, inductive, and fact-ridden treatise.

What we learn from philosopher Descartes...

A write-up deviating from the consideration of the exact level of audience will fall flat like the discourses of René Descartes. Descartes was a French philosopher who used to deliver his sermons to large number of people. His maid-servant was a wise lady and she, too, used to attend his lecture-sessions. Descartes was, however, missing that lady in his recent lectures. Therefore, he once asked her when he saw her at home: *"Why aren't you attending my lectures these days? Lost interest in them now?"*

"*It's not so*", replied the lady, "*but I feel bored.*"

"*But why?*"

The lady remarked: "*Because I don't understand why you repeat the same theories and propositions over and over again?*"

Descartes smiled and said: "*That's because I want even the most foolish of the audience grasp my point*".

"By the time the foolish grasp your point", the lady turned to go, *"all the wise people have already left the hall."*

This is exactly what a writer must know. For whom is he writing? Is it that he is considering his reader to be less witted, unwise, foolish? Is he using too many capitalized words, emphasized italics, exclamation marks, etc., to 'point out' to the reader that he does not trust his or her wisdom to understand the things the way he wants? Is he, like Descartes, repeating something so overly that it repels the wise reader?

When we imagine deeply and "preview" our readers in our mental image, many problems are solved and we are able to write well for the right group of readers.

Imagination also arouses empathy...

Suppose, a very close contact of yours has lost his or her mother and it is now imperative for you to write a condolence letter. There may be hundreds of condolence letters being sent to that family, all using expressions like *"I was deeply aggrieved to know about the sudden demise of your beloved mother ...."* What is your letter going to be like? Can it be so empathetic that it will touch the hearts of the family members?

The use of imagination in such contexts is to put you (yourself) in the place of that family. This is called empathy. Suppose you are that very person who has suffered the loss of his mother. Be in his place, imbibe his grief in your own heart, drink his tears in your own eyes, feel his loss in you own inner world.

Remember, the only difference between an ordinary actor and a great actor is that of empathy. An ordinary actor 'plays' his character, a great actor 'lives' his character. The same difference applies between an ordinary writer and a great writer. To play the character of a tramp, a great actor becomes that character and lives his dreams and aspirations, lacks and sufferings. Therefore, he does not have to 'act', what he does becomes a reality on the screen. A good and great writer 'becomes his reader' and whatever, then, he thinks and writes establishes a touch-screen relation with his readers.

Therefore, before sending a condolence letter, know the socio-religious moorings of that family. Death is not a tea-party; it is a deep-rooted emotional occasion. Your words must reflect emotional feeling.

In every religion, there are different writings and teachings about death that become the core values of that family. They use different phrases and expressions for the person who has passed away. For example, a Hindu '*ascends to heaven*' after death, a Baha'i soul '*rests in the Abha kingdom*', etc.

Starting the condolence letter with appropriate holy text from the religious book respected by that family, using the right phrases and terms, and reflecting the right type of belief in your letter (for example, if a family does not believe in reincarnation, don't write: "*May in each birth I find her as my aunt...*") will go a long way in making your condolence message a memorable one! And, then, it is not just about a condolence letter but all about kinds of writing – developing an empathetic attitude guides us well what the contents of our writing should be.

Ten Top Tips

1. Observation and imagination are two words that lead to powerful writing.
2. Observation and imagination are not just useful for us to be great writers but they also help express our ideas in a better way.
3. Observation and imagination are two aspects of the same coin.
4. Everything tells something about itself, if we but observe and listen.
5. A small piece of news, a negligible object in our surrounding, can reveal many hidden truths if we just observe and imagine.
6. Imagination helps us develop a rapport with our reader.
7. Imagining the potential reader guides to adapt our writing as per his/her/their level and aptitude.
8. A good writer must always trust the wisdom of his reader.
9. Imagination arouses empathy.
10. A great writer 'becomes' his reader and then whatever he writes establishes a touch-screen relation with his reader.

Exercise 5

Match your answers with those given on the ANSWER PAGE. Give yourself 2 marks for each correct answer.

1. **Which group rightly describes Kishore Massab?**
    A. Poor, young, handsome, distasteful, modern.
    B. Poor, young, handsome, sober, traditional.
    C. Clever, liar, rustic, proud, selfish.
    D. Simple, uncivilized, useless, poor, homeless.

2. **"Maneuvering a sobriety on his face which crisscrossed his handsome and innocent looks" - what does it mean in context with Kishore Massab?**
    A. He was a hypocrite.
    B. He was looking funny trying to be serious.
    C. The sober gesture was opposed to his facial beauty and Innocence.
    D. He was handsome and innocent but his situation made him sober.

3. **In what way 'observation' and 'imagination' are twins or two aspects of the same coin?**
    A. Imagination cannot be developed without observation and without imagination observation has no dimensions.
    B. Imagination is useless without observation.
    C. Observation leads to imagination and imagination leads to observation.
    D. Those who imagine have no time to observe and those who observe imagine nothing.

4. **How can you develop keen rapport with your reader?**
    A. By writing everything so simply that even a foolish reader can understand.
    B. By constantly putting emphasis, capitalization, exclamation marks, etc.
    C. By writing only such things as most readers want to read.
    D. By keeping the potential reader in view while writing.

5. **What lesson could Descartes have learnt from his maid-servant?**
    A. When dealing with foolish audience, be foolish like them.
    B. When dealing with wise audience, don't act foolish.
    C. Be specific to your readers/audience and trust in their wisdom.

D. There is no need to care who understands and who fails to understand our points; we said what we said.

6. How does imagination help us develop empathy?
    A. It lets us 'be' and 'feel' like our reader.
    B. It lets us find details about our reader.
    C. It lets us be kind and sympathetic to someone.
    D. It helps us write a good condolence letter.

Assignments 5

1. Here are some statements as if some objects or qualities are talking to you. Write against each statement who might have said that. Choose the objects or the qualities from the box below. (***Check answers on the ANSWER PAGE***)

   I. Like a beautiful, dark-complexioned fairy I am alighting down on the earth from the dusky sky spreading my dense, black hair.

   II. I am your close friend who lets you put your fingers on my keys and write your thoughts whatsoever. You can see your words on my screen as your face in the mirror. I keep everything inside like a trusted friend.

   III. I am a tiny creature lost in weaving my own world. My world is a snare for those who come in it. This world is also the same. But King Bruce took a bold lesson from me – Try, try again.

   IV. I am the most desired thing that came out of the Pandora's Box. One can live a miserable life, suffer all hardships and yet look into my eyes for a bright tomorrow.

   V. I am someone whom you trust, for whose arrival you wait. I share your joys and sorrows and if I am sincere I am the best boon for anyone.

2. Read the following newspaper headings. Imagine the 'inside story' and write a short paragraph on <u>any one</u> of them.

   • Doctors found asleep in the emergency ward at night

   • First operation with the use of Robot done successfully at AIIMS, New Delhi

- Heavy rainfall, traffic halted for one hour in suburban Mumbai
- Thousands of children in Ghana dying due to starvation – A UN Report
- Colourful cultural evening held to commemorate Canada Day

   Spider   Friend   Evening

   Hope   Computer

3. Write a condolence letter to your father's friend, Sardar Harkeerat Singh, who is a Sikh businessman whose mother has just passed away.

   (*Model answer given on ANSWER PAGE*)

4. Observe and write at least 3 qualities of the following:

   Your mother _____

   Your best friend _____

   Your personal computer or television _____

   Your pet dog or cat _____

   Your teacher _____

Chapter 6

The Treasure of Silence

This silence says ... a volcano is about to erupt.

– Anonymous

This huge, immeasurable universe is an epitome of silence, even though every moment a new galaxy is being created, countless stars dismantle and submerge in an abysmal depth like 'Black Hole'. There are unimaginable numbers of 'worlds' like our earth -- each of them witnessing creation and destruction every instant, producing noise and collision, breakage and friction, thuds and thunders of incredible volumes. And yet, in camparison to all this noise, the universe is immensely silent in its wholeness ... so silent that in its deep tranquility you can feel your own heartbeat!

The most powerful voice is silence. Anyone who desires to acquire a good penmanship and become a well versed writer, must do so by tapping the illimitable resources of the world unseen. He must rely on the whispers of the 'hidden angels' for the loveliest and greatest ideas that humankind could ever have. And to listen to these 'whispers' one has to learn to be silent.

Different frequencies of our mind...

As it is scientifically proven, the conscious or logical mind hardly has 5 percent capacity of the total mind power. The remaining 95 percent lies hidden beyond its active grasp. The main reason for this limit of the conscious mind is that it works under the influences of the '***Beta***' waves which have a frequency of 14 Hz (Hertz) and above. On this frequency, the mind is not able to stop and ponder deeply over subtler, finer and more profound currents of thoughts. We are living in a cosmic ocean, so to say, in which there's a continuous flow of thought vibrations, and all is connected to each other through a universal mind. Renowned psychologist Carl Jung has said and proved that we are living in a world of 'collective unconsciousness' in which each individual is connected with the other and can draw the feelings and experiences from the vast accumulation of universal knowledge. We know this is true because each one of us must have such experiences when suddenly we became sad, without any apparent reason, and soon news came about an earthquake or a heart-rending incident in some other part of the world.

As we know, some waves are on the surface of the ocean but there are also deep-flowing waves. In the same way, there is a conscious level on which we are living, and there are also deeper levels of sub or super consciousnesses which can only be felt when we depart from the noisy surface of our active life. We make our ordinary, usual and daily decisions using this Beta level of mind. It does not need any in-depth consideration. To be exact, thoughts occurring in the conscious mind are 'thoughts on the surface'.

Then, there is an '*Alpha*' state of the mind with a electro vibration frequency of 7-14 Hz. At this frequency, it can 'catch more subtle thoughts'. In this state, we are 'semi' or 'sub' conscious, that is, we are half awake and half asleep. One half of our mind is connected to the 'deep' currents from where it is picking precious 'gems', and the other half of our mind is connected to the 'surface' where it brings out these gems for our use. This is the state where ideas are born, in a relaxed, silent mood.

Even deeper state of mind is that of '*Theta*' waves with a frequency of 4-7 Hz. This is a sleeping, dream-like state. In other words, we are not conscious at all but, later, when this state is over, we can recollect some 'glimpses' of our unconscious state. Many solutions of life that could not be solved consciously are often solved in the Alpha and Theta states of mind. Scientists have described these states of mind as follows:

- Our visualization and creativity is heightened.
- These frequencies are closer with the frequencies of the earth's magnetic field (9.4 Hz) and so we are much balanced with the gravitational energy.
- We feel peace and calmness and, hence, have more control over our thoughts.
- More amount of Serotonin is released – a neurotransmitter that makes us feel good by eliminating anxiety, depression, nausea, migraine and other disturbing mental conditions.
- There's increased harmony between the mind and body.

- Imagination and intuition are intensified.
- Our mind becomes more receptive and feels highly inspired from within.

The silence zones of our mind...

The evident reason for these stimulated and empowered conditions of mind is, in fact, silence. Normally, human ears cannot listen to sounds below 20 Hz. Thus, even when we are wide-awake, in the full-conscious Beta state of mind, we miss out many sounds. But in Alpha, Theta and Delta states our propensity to sound increases. They are the *"silence zones"* of our mind. There we can hear the whispering of 'angels', to use a metaphoric term. As long as we are awake, in the conscious state of mind, we are in "noise" and unrest. Even if we are ourselves silent, the noise pollution around us is reaching our domain and preventing us from realizing the calmness essential for deeper susceptibilities.

Many great scientists, like **Thomas Alva Edison** and **Einstein**, used to escape to privacy and siesta, to come out later with fresher ideas and nobler thoughts. Famous author, R.L. Stevenson, greatly relied on the subconscious power and used to sleep dictating his mind to 'bring out a new thriller' for him. He described the world of dreams as a *"small theater of the brain which we keep brightly lighted all night long."* Bill Gates practices the same inner silence that yields him innovative ideas and Henry Ford even employed some people on high salaries only to 'think calmly' and do nothing else.

Dreams that float in our mind in the state of utmost **'Theta'** silence reveal strange worlds to us and answer the most unsolvable problems of our life. The symbolic languages of the dream have helped many writers, inventors and ordinary people. The proofs and facts are so many that one full book, oh nay, many volumes of books can be written just on the topic of dreams and the ideas inspired into many souls.

We all know, for example, how **Paul McCartney** composed the tune for his popular Beatles song "*Yesterday*" (1965) after 'feeling' the particular music in his dream. The story of Elias Howe, the inventor of sewing machine, is popular. Elias did not exactly know how to develop a machine-operated needle and how to fix it with a hole-point suitable to stitch clothes. Traditional needles were different and would not work. When he gave up all his efforts, he saw that bizarre dream in which he was beset by aboriginal people dancing around him with spears which, as Elias observed in his dream, had holes on the point-side, and this gave him the required idea for the sewing machine. **Abraham Lincoln**, the great President of America, clearly saw his own death just 10 days before he was actually assassinated. World renowned mathematician, **Srinivasa Ramanujan**, admitted that most of his theorems and solutions were inspired by his dreams. **Madame Walker**, the first female self-made American millionaire (as per the Guinness Book of World Records), carved her fortune out of a dream. The lady suffered a chronic hair-loss and no medicine proved to be of any affect. Then she saw a dream in which a mystic African formula was given to her for her hair. When she got up, she concocted the formula and it worked! That is how she established a big cosmetic company and minted money as fast as her hair grew. A British engineer trying to build a mighty bridge in Allahabad over the confluence of two rivers repeatedly failed to do so. Each time he laid the pillars, they were washed away. Then his wife told him about a dream she had the previous night in which he (the engineer) was wading through the river confluence wearing typical shoes with flat and semi-arched frontage. A new insight glimmered in the engineer's eyes and he erected pillars exactly like the shoes described by his wife, and the bridge was successfully built and endures even now.

Thus, the creative power of the subconscious mind reflected in our dreams, inspirations or intuitions is truly the power of silence. The most powerful feelings are silent. Yet, in our daily life, silence is the most missing element. In buses, in trams, trains and taxis, even in elevators, in market places and prohibited zones like a library, we have only 'talking people'. Nobody inclines to look out of the window and see the argentine splendor of a bright sun, or feel the calmness that prevails in the domain of nature, or watch the sparkling colors of the flowers and the butterfly. Talking ... talking ... talking .... and when old people are talking, even children go on chattering, and we say: "*It's natural for them.*" Why is it natural to talk all the time and make noise? Why is not natural to be serene?

When Swami Vivekananda was on his trip to Japan, he observed during a train journey how Japanese children were so calm and quiet.

It was an unusual experience for the great Indian monk and he even thought that this calmness in the minds of children might be detrimental to their development. Since then decades have passed and Japan has advanced more progressively than any other country – a silent progress, a salient progress.

To be silent is a prerequisite for a good writer – whether you want to be a great literary writer of the stature of Milton or Gorky or simply a good student or office correspondent. Your success in writing will greatly depend on how less you talk and how much you observe and listen. If you talk too much, you observe too less because, as the proverb goes: *"the man who opens his mouth, closes his eyes."*

The value of inner silence...

Remember one more thing: it's not sufficient to observe and listen to others only. Listen to yourself, too. It seems that we all shun silence out of some fear. Even if we have 'shut out' external noise, the internal noise and tumult is still reigning. In a minute, countless thoughts and anxieties pass through our mind. We fear that silence will lead us to an 'island of solitude' within us and this seems to be a scary situation. All noise – inside or outside – is a disorderly expression of fear, insecurity, envy, hatred, anxiety and chaos. Here's a story from the life of Lord Buddha. He had many devotees and, at the same time, malicious people who envied him. Once when he was in deep meditation, one such person came, stopped by him, observed him hatefully for some time, came near him and slapped on his face. Buddha opened his eyes, looked calmly at the scornful fellow, smiled and asked: *"Anything else you have to say?"* It is clear that Buddha interpreted his assault as an 'expression' and asked if he had to 'say' anything more. Every expression of noise tends to say *"we are afraid to be our true self"*.

All of us are too noisy to listen to our own self or, more aptly, the truth is that we don't want to listen to our 'self'. As **Hermann Hesse** said: **"Nothing in the world is more distasteful to a man than to take the path that leads to himself."** But once we follow the road to our own self, we start listening to the whispers of our own conscience, the subtle voices of our own inmost depth, and this leads to self-realization and perfection. It is not sufficient just to shut our mouth and turn off that tape-recorder. The inner restlessness, fickle-mindedness, mood swings, tempers and tantrums, wild passions and animalistic nuisances, too, need to be conquered.

Life has its own tests and trials, tempests and turmoils, but he who stands like a deep-rooted tree – nonchalant and non-affected – acquires that composure of mind which makes a thoughtful writer. One does not become a writer just by mastering some styles and dictions, themes and topics, but by developing a 'school of thought' of his own out of his time-tested principles. People know that when they are reading **Tolstoy** they are to enter a world of thoughtful compassion, a profound spirituality with a lofty sense of service to mankind, a moral world of humane emotions. On the other hand, when they have a book of **Vladimir Nabokov** in their hands, they don't expect the same.

Each writer is first known for his thought and later for his styles. And to chisel your thought, you have to conquer your petty fears, lusts, doubts, greeds, uncertainties, etc., and you've to rise above the rest. You cannot do this without standing aloof from the ups and downs of life. You cannot do this without developing a profound silence inside you – truly something like a black hole – that sucks up every atom of minutest nature in its unfathomable depth, or like an ocean that even a hundred rivers will silently settle into it without disturbing its peace.

So what should a writer do? Should he sever all his connections from the human society? Should he not be affected by the sparks of lights and spots of darknesses in his life?

No doubt, a writer is a human being but he is also a fashioner of human minds. Somewhere, he has to stand above the rest or he cannot be a guide and a thought provocateur. Misfortunes befall and people cry and sob, but the one who is the guardian, in spite of his sore-vexed heart, finds a corner to wipe his tears, pat on the shoulders of the mourners and say: "*Life's like that; be patient*". Every writer, if he truly wants to rise above the rest, must develop his personality in like manners. Even when the colours of life change, day passes into night, clamours of a hopeless world test his serenity of mind, times try to shatter him into pieces, he holds himself and whispers to his soul: "*Life's like that; be patient*".

How to develop inner silence...

A very important thing to be noted is: silence is not an action but an attitude. There are people who are living in outwardly silent atmosphere and yet they feel heavily disturbed inside. On the contrary, there are people who usually have to live in a noisy circumference and they are still calm. In the same way, silence and peace has not to do so much with people around you. Observing silence and inner peace does not mean that we need to live a solitary life in a jungle. It is just a feeling of *'being oneself'*, self-contained, self-controlled, happy inside, content inside. With such a state of mind, we don't feel alienated and lonely. We talk, we socialize, we participate in any event but then we return to our "*inner island*" of peace.

So, the first step is to think of silence as something already inside and then feel this silence. Lord Buddha, in very brief and yet deeply pregnant words, has thus shown us the path and virtue of inner peace: *"Meditate. Live purely. Be quiet. Do your work with mastery. Like the moon, come out from behind the clouds and shine."*

Anahat Naad - The Supreme Silence: The *Big Bang* theory establishes that this universe was created billions of years ago and it is, since then, in the process of expansion and evolution, still cooling down and settling. Scientists explain this phenomenon as *'life appearing out as a singularity'*. Before this 'Big Bang' there was no time, no space, no matter, no energy. The Bible says: *"In the beginning was the Word and the Word was with God"* (*John 1: 1, 3*). It is believed that the 'sound' of the Big Bang is still there in the universe. Spiritually speaking, the Word of God is continuously echoing in the universe since it was created. In the Yogic philosophy of Hinduism, this phenomenon is termed as *Anāhat Nād* that means 'unbeaten sound', because this sound is not caused by an external friction, striking or beating of two objects as is usual with all other sounds. It is a perpetual, self-generated and self-sustained sound. For this reason, *Anāhat Nād* is also referred to as 'Song of God', 'Primal Sound', or 'Soundless Sound'. And even though it is 'sound', it is so pitched and set on such pleasing frequency that we experience it as perfect silence. Hence, it is also known as "supreme silence".

Whatever it may be, we are plunged into a sea of tranquility. Meditation is wonderful for realizing this tranquility inside our own self, and has already been dealt with in the previous chapter (*Connect to The Source*). Moreover, there are several *yogic* devices – including *asanas, mudras,* and *pranayam* – which have been found very useful in promoting inner peace as they enable us to perceive the *Anāhat Nād*. The purpose here is not to go into *Yogic* details. Any reader can easily find suitable books and resources on Yoga and learn more. The method which I use is a simple blend of meditation + shambhavi mudra + pranayam which was taught to me by my uncle, Mr. G.M. Bhatta, an associate and friend of late Dr. Phulgenda Sinha, Director, Yoga Institute of Washington (USA) and Indian Institute of Yoga, Patna, and I have found it convenient and useful for myself.

To experience this "supreme silence" inside you, follow these practices daily for at least 10 minutes, preferably in early morning and/or before retiring at night, in a peaceful atmosphere.

STEPS

1. Sit in a relaxed but firm position with your bust straight and eyes closed. For some minutes, just concentrate on your breathing. Breathe as deeply as you can but don't be fast or hasty. The body must be still. After some time, breathe slowly, gradually effortlessly.
2. Plug your ears with your thumbs and pay attention to the inner sound. You may hear a continuous sizzling, echoing or sensational sound – something like the chirping of crickets in a silent night.
3. Your eyes are already closed. Now, the balls of the eyes should be raised slightly up inside your eye-sockets. Also, press your eyes lightly with your index or middle fingers. There should be no strain on the eyes. Inwardly focus your entire attention on the middle of the eyebrows.
4. While still attentive to the inner sound, imagine any good picture (preferably a spiritual symbol like a flower, a candle or light, etc.) and concentrate on the image. Thus, you are busy in two – and only two – activities: listening to the inner sound and focusing on the inward image. Though your thoughts will wander in the beginning, gradually you will succeed.
5. Remain in this condition as long as you feel comfortable. Now remove your thumbs and free your ears. You are now exposed to outwardly sound. Try to hear everything ... even the farthest and minutest of sounds that you can perceive. Remove the fingers and free your eyes, too. Don't open the eyes suddenly but slowly and slowly.
6. Remain peaceful in this condition for some seconds and then resume your normalcy.

These steps are especially important as they activate the Ajna Chakra, one of the seven major *"Chakras"* (wheels) or 'energy-points' of the human body as envisioned in the Indian philosophy of Yoga. The Ajna Chakra (the wheel of command), positioned between the eyebrows, is just below the apex chakra, namely the Sahasrar Chakra (the wheel of Lotus). The Ajna Chakra, depicted with two petals of lotus -- the spiritually symbolic flower – stands for the point of intermingling between the conscious and the subconscious, invigorates meditative state of the mind, infuses intuition, and promotes sleep and mental balance.

<u>Sky - The Abode of Peace</u>: The sky is the abode of peace … the endless space where all sounds dissolve like rivers in the sea. Bringing the sky in our imagination instantly reduces our tension and induces tranquility. Any time when you desire to feel your inner peace, sit in your privacy, be relaxed and close your eyes. Try to visualize a clear sky with some pleasant clouds floating freely in its width, or imagine a peaceful sky of midnight with shining stars or a brilliant moon. Imagine the sky over the ocean and see the end where the ocean and the sky meet. Let your mind make any combination of the sky and its properties. Let it imagine that you are flying in a balloon or in a magical, fairytale sky-boat, or just you have your own wings and you are flying higher and higher – carefree of the limits of the earth and bold to explore a new world.

These visualizations will not only induce inner peace but -- if practiced regularly, devotedly and for several months -- will also free one's subconscious mind from the inexplicable fears of confined places (*claustrophobia*), fear of height (*acrophobia*), fear of loneliness (*autophobia*), etc.

In brief, silence is peace, and peace – more importantly, inner peace -- is essential for creativity. You will gradually come to realize that silence has many things in store for you:

- Silence helps our mind to stay in a relaxed state and this, eventually, increases the latent capacities of mind.
- When we are silent, we are good observers and learn more about people and things.
- It is the nature of mind to be busy always. When we are talking and making noise, or feeling anxious inside, the mind is busy and not free for creative ideas.

- Silence gives us inner peace and a lot of freedom to our conscious mind to interact with our subconscious mind and come out with precious gems of thoughts.
- Silence balances the rhythm of the body and harmonizes mind-body coherence.
- Silence is such a vital attribute for inner growth, peace, creativity and spiritual progress that all great religions have underlined its importance.

Ten Top Tips

1. Silence lets us listen to the whispers of the 'hidden angels' for the profoundest and greatest ideas.
2. We are living in a cosmic ocean of thought vibrations – all connected to each other through a universal mind.
3. The power of the subconscious mind is, in fact, the power of silence.
4. Silence helps our mind to stay relaxed and thus enhance its latent capacities.
5. To be silent is a prerequisite for being a good writer.
6. Each writer is first known for his thought – and thought takes shape when one develops a profound silence in his or her being.
7. Silence is an attitude of the mind. If we are peaceful within, outwardly noise can disturb us but a little.
8. We are immersed in a deep ocean of cosmic silence (some call it the Anāhat Nād and some name it the 'Song of God') – meditating on this supreme silence induces inner peace.
9. The sky is the abode of peace ... the endless space where all sounds dissolve. Imagining the sky – and clouds, stars, etc. – promotes inner silence and even removes many phobias.
10. Silence allows us to be good observers and listeners – two essential qualities for successful writers.

Exercise 6

Match your answers with those given on the ANSWER PAGE. Give yourself 2 marks for each correct answer.

1. The conscious mind is associated with _____ rays which have a frequency of 14 Hz and above.
   - A. Beta
   - B. Theta
   - C. Delta
   - D. Alpha

2. Which mind is responsible for making decisions?
   - A. Conscious
   - B. Unconscious
   - C. Subconscious
   - D. Super Conscious

3. How can we 'listen to ourselves'?
   - A. Through a sonometer
   - B. By practicing inner silence
   - C. Through planned dreams
   - D. By talking constantly with others

4. What is 'claustrophobia'?
   - A. Fear of deep places
   - B. Fear of height
   - C. Fear of confined places
   - D. Fear of water

5. Why is it important for a writer to rise above the trials and turmoils of life?
   - A. Because he/she must develop into a saint.
   - B. Because a good writer ought to be heartless and insensitive.
   - C. Because life is like that and there's no need to care anything.
   - D. Because he must attain stability of mind and thought.

6. What are the 'Chakras' according to Yoga?
   - A. Wheels of fortune
   - B. Glands excreting some chemicals
   - C. Energy centers in human body
   - D. Points of acupressure

Assignments 6

1. Did you ever have a dream you still remember? Give a detailed description of your dream: when did you have that dream? What was special about it? Why do you still remember that dream?

2. Write a short note (in about 300 words) on a writer of your choice. Do you like that writer for his or her thoughts and philosophy? What is special about his or her vision which attracts you?

3. Make a list of at least 20 words – all related to the sky.

   (*Model answer given on ANSWER PAGE*)

4. Similarly, now make a list of at least 20 words – all related to your kitchen.

Chapter 7

Gather Your Thoughts

I think and that is all that I am.

- Wayne Dyer

Average people have something in common which keeps them 'average' and ordinary. Extraordinary people also have something in common and so they have an 'extra' added before them. The difference in the worlds of these two can be summed up in one sentence – Ordinary people mould their thoughts as per reality and extraordinary people mould their realities as per their thoughts. The 'reality' that is visible to the 'ordinary' is that iron sinks in water and therefore, they 'thought' that iron can never float. But for an 'extraordinary' **Archimedes**, the 'thought' of the '***law of buoyancy***' which paved the way for an unforeseen 'reality' when big iron ships traversed through seas. The 'ordinary' laughed at the **Wright Brothers** because the 'reality' suggested them that no 'thought' can be entertained which says that a man can ever fly. The 'extraordinary' followed the Wright's dreams and now the realities are visible in the sky everyday. Mighty and meaningful inventions and ideas spring forth from such minds as they 'think' beyond realities. A good, successful writer is also the one who believes, first and foremost, in his or her thoughts. Thoughts are your weapons, sharpen them and keep them ready. Nobody values the beauty of a sheath or ornaments on a sword more than the sharpness of the sword itself. Likewise, if your thought is dull or impotent, scattered and vague, all amounts of your labour in brandishing occult words and intricate styles will go in vain.

Gather your thoughts. Make your thoughts so concentrated, mighty, clear, sharp and grave that when a reader is going through your novel, poem, essay or article, he exclaims: *"how touching, how powerful these thoughts and feelings are!"* So enraptured does he become with the beauty and marvel of your creative thrust that his entire attention is withdrawn from your punctuation and spellings, syntax and phrases, words and axioms and everything that is no more important than a mere topping on the dessert. By bringing this prominence of thought, you will notice that the right words, flavour, style and pitch naturally followed as fragrance follows the wind.

Thought should be clear and powerful. Thought is the first thing to influence human minds. **Mahatma Gandhi** was not a versed writer but his thought on truth and non-violence were so clear and potent that it uprooted the mighty British Empire from India. His autobiographical book "***My Experiments with Truth***" does not reflect any other beauty and charm than the sincerity of his thought. One of the most revolutionizing personalities of modern history, **Karl Marx**, whose books such as '***Das Capital***' influenced a multitude, was not popular for his writing style but for the clarity of his thought and mission contained in this all-time famous slogan: "**Workers of the World, Unite. You have nothing to lose but your chains!**"

The value of 'thought' for a writer...

Would you like to read a writer who is praising materialism in one book and in his next book he is eulogizing spiritualism? Would you respect and value a writer who is today an atheist and tomorrow a pagan? What impression would you get from a writer whose piece of work has all qualities but you can't guess what he wants to say?

Thought has two 'place-values' in a writer's life -- and it need not be reminded that throughout this book the term "writer" does not denote only a professional writer, poet, author, essayist, journalist or such people but even a student, an office correspondent, and any person who is 'writing' something for a result or gain. However, the first place-value of thought, as described below, is surely highly important for an established writer.

The first place-value of 'thought' is a <u>generic</u> place value and is related to your personality. When a reader picks up a book from the book-stand, he is picking up a '*thought*' that corresponds to his intellectual demand. And he knows that a certain writer would be able to cater to his mind's thirst. For him or her, a writer becomes an 'embodiment' of certain ideals and thought-patterns and this is what attunes a writer with his reader. It is incumbent therefore that a writer's thoughts should be as solid and time-tested as any consumer product may be. He should have a 'brand of thought' ... a quality brand ... a non-changeable brand ... a reliable brand. Remember: it is your thought that sells your writing, other things are ancillaries.

The second place-value of 'thought' is <u>specific</u> and relates to your writing. This value of thought gives shape to your 'product' – your write-up in any form. Your fiction or non-fiction, letter or article, news or report, assignment or project work -- all must be woven around certain 'thoughts'. What words are to be chosen, what *style* is to be adopted, what the *structure* of the sentences should be like, should we use idiomatic or plain *language* – all these things are like servants of a King. Where the King (thought) will go, they must follow.

Make your thoughts clear by focusing on the subject for a length of time. Contemplate in a cool but curious manner and not in haste or excitement. You have already read in the previous chapters that you have a subconscious power and receptivity for intuitions and these powers work when you are relaxed, not tense. Focus your thought on these four things. Subjects may vary but, as a basic rule, these four points will serve as a helipad for your thoughts to take-off.

- What the overall subject is (on which you have to write)? – Think on the 'subject' and its outlines. For example, the subject on which you have to write is description of a historic conference of your club or society or your School's Annual Function, your office's momentous gathering or retreat. When was it? What was special in it? Who were there? What were the impacts? How it started? Focus on introductory thoughts.
- What are the ingredients of the subject? – Think about the flavours and stuff. Try to give details which will arouse interest, promote intimacy with the subject, and tell about the striking features. For example, you may give an account of how the function began and how the participants reflected their zeal. Any songs? Drama? Cultural shows? What were the elements that you or others liked the most? In brief, take care of the emotional parts.
- What are the details? - Emotions are okay but facts should also be there. Who organized the programme? Why? How many participants were there? Who were the Guests of Honour, keynote speakers? In brief, what did they say? Who got what prize? What about the media coverage? Was the event telecasted on TV? When, on which TV? Physical arrangements, light and sound, main volunteers/performers, the conclusion.
- What it means in the end? – Think about your concluding remarks. You cannot end a write-up with a thud and go away. In a short

paragraph you must write something touching, something like a message that goes into the head of the reader and makes him or her feel a sense of relief, hope, humor or anything emphatic. For example, the end-lines can say: *"Words can never exactly portray the fervor and warmth of this dazzling event. Even more important was to see so many enthusiastic people under a roof, in their colorful dresses and with dreamful hearts. How sad to see them departing in the end but how great that again we will meet ... the next year – same place, same venue, and with the same zeal!"*

Believe in your vision ...

Every thought appears in the beginning as a blurred, vague vision – like an embryo – not very clear, solid or well-shaped but you know you've 'conceived' something. That's your vision, follow it. That's your guiding light, beaconing to the right shore. A time will come when it would be clear and whole.

When Napoleon Bonaparte was but a child, a world map was spread before him and with a pencil he was ticking country after country. His mother asked: *'What are you doing?"* Still lost in observing the map and scanning with his keen eyes places after places, Napoleon replied: *"When I'm grown up, I will conquer all these nations"*. The child had a vision. He had no knowledge of warfare at that time, he didn't have the faintest idea of the political or geographical conditions of the nations he was idealizing to overcome, nor did he know about the valor and military equipages of the kings and rulers he would be thwarting tomorrow. <u>But he had a vision and he believed in it</u>.

Carefully chisel your thought, the vision that is coming from 'inside' you. Believe in it and hold it firmly, as a feeble plant is held firmly by a wood-stick, in the frame of your mind till it coalesces into a solid content. A writer is born in your mind.

Beginning with a thought ...

When you have to write something – whatever it may be – like a *literary* Napoleon Bonaparte, sit relaxed with a small card or a piece of paper, not bigger than a postcard, and draw out a map of your idea. Gather your main thoughts. If your thought is clear, it essentially has to be brief, expressed in short paragraphs. That is the essence of your thought ... the rest is elaboration.

When you think deeply and focus on the subject, an outline should appear in your vision, may be the next morning if not instantly. Sometimes clearer images are created when we think on ... think on ... and then go to sleep. A flashlight makes things clearer for you to begin with. For example, you have an idea of a story – THE DARK SHADOW. It's a detective novel, and is based on what you have initially viewed it, its thought summary can be written like this:

As soon as the dark night envelopes the vibrant city in its peaceful embrace, a dark shadow walks out as a 'wicked silhouette' amidst the sleeping sky-scrapers. In the morning newspapers, again the same horrifying news is repeated: 'Three more women in the age-groups of 30-35 years have been killed by the strange murderer'. Who is he? Why does he kill women of a certain age-group only ... almost in the same manner ... with no trace? To find the answer to these questions, read further.

Thus, this is the basic outline of a thought from which the warps and wefts of your novel will be woven.

Developing the thought...

Now, as a second step, you have to develop the thought. A constant focus on the subject matter will help you again. When we develop a thought, three distinctive parts evolve – the beginning (or the head), the middle (or the body) and the end (or the tail). How we start on a subject matter is its head. How we put in the details and broad descriptions is the body. How we finish up is the tail. All these three parts should be smoothly interwoven so that they form one healthy whole.

As the word 'focus' implies, we cannot focus on a broad area at a time. In a given moment, focus must be on a small concentrated area. You first focus only on the 'overall thought' of your detective story – THE DARK SHADOW – and write down a small summary. Now, you have to focus only on one thing: How to begin the story? To begin a story or any other write-up is the main challenge. It must begin with an interesting note, in a way that pulls the reader to the next line, to the next paragraph, to the next chapter. When you will focus constantly, your subconscious mind will again come to your help – instantly or later. Some hints, some ideas, some images will appear in your mind. For example, you may see the image of a deserted house ... the house in flames ... a man inside the house beset by fire ... screaming for help ... and a ghastly woman in her thirties with a fire-brand in her hand ... revenge in her eyes ... STOP. Note it down. Try to read the symbols, weave the story out of this stuff. You've got a beginning. Your story will begin with the scene of a burning house – and the revengeful lady could be the first fiancée of that man he deserted. And now the spirit of that man who met with a tragic death is out to take revenge and he is looking for that woman who killed him and, in the process he ends up, killing several women of the same age.

Get ready to slough off ...

A snake casts off its slough when its body outgrows. New cells replace outworn cells. You conceived a preliminary idea and evolved your writing. Now, when you will proceed further, you will find that things are taking a new shape. The characters you initially devised, the matters you wanted to elucidate, the climaxes you previously thought, the scenes you envisioned in the beginning are all blending into a new form, moving into a different direction. Let it be so as long as you feel good about this shift. Most great writers began to write a children story and what they actually wrote became a globe-turning book. When you are writing from your heart, it happens naturally. When an engineer constructs a bridge or a towering building, some supporting structures are built to support the columns and give base to the roofs. Later, when the solid construction is built, these supports are no longer needed.

All that you have to do is to begin with an idea and then let it loose. There is a mind above your mind ... just mind it and go on.

The power of thought: wherefrom it comes?

There are more things to be considered about the 'thought' because it is clear that the most powerful ingredient of your writing is the thought. How a thought becomes more powerful than the other? How can you compete in the market with so many blooming writers? If you will visit different websites, read books and consult professionals such as literary agents and others who have a 'say' in the world of literature, you will hear too many discouraging thoughts and you will instantly decide to give up writing as a profession. They will tell you about everything you '*lack*' and nothing that you 'possess'. They will tell you that the market is tight, publishers are stingy, trends are this and that, there is a global slump in the book market as electronic media is gaining an upper hand, good writing means years of patience and practice, and sooooooo many appalling things that you will have no alternative left than to quit. But now, after reading these passages, go and tell them that the thought comes from a fire and that fire is your desire. Tell them that the way may be congested for imitating foxes but once the lion of high spirits is out, all will give way to him. Tell them that your writing is great because YOU think it is great and not because they announce its evaluation. Be like **George Bernard Shaw**. One of his dramas did not fair well at the theatres. Hardly some scores of people turned up to watch the show, and some ill-hearted 'friends' came to ask him how successful the drama was. G.B. Shaw had his usual lighted smile and said: "***The drama was quite successful, but the audience failed***". Always feel great value for your writing. The critics might have failed but have faith that your thought is powerful. It is not the point that we should not consider healthy criticisms, it is not the point that there is no room for improvement in our writing, the point is: I should not be swayed away by other's judgments and think lowly of my creativity as long as it sound good, pure and superb in my own views. The <u>four</u> touchstones on which you can prove the viability and vitality of your thought are the following:

1. **Simplicity:** Your thought should be simple and not so complicated that only you or a few others can understand it. If you are given a chance to explain about your thought to a high school student, you should have no problem in doing so. Then, it means, your thought is capable of moving millions. Great writers never wrote about complicated matters but rather about simple and touching aspects of human lives. Read any writer whom you and all the people consider great – they wrote about that simple love that bloomed in the silent corners of the garden of our heart, hatred and envy that sprang like thorns below the velvety roses of tenderness, about the traits of 'God' and the 'Demon' both living inside us. Their stories were woven from the textures of our tears and smiles, hopes and glooms, valour and timidities, humours and wraths. In "***Kabuliwala***", ***Tagore*** told us

the simple story of an Afghani nut-seller's love for a small girl who reminded him of his own daughter, but told it in such a way that tears rolled out of our eyes. In "***Three Questions***", ***Tolstoy*** did not deal with any superhuman questions but a simple inquisitiveness of a king who wanted to know what's the right time to start doing something, who were the right people to listen to and what was the most important work to be done. And the story weaves events leading the king, in a natural way, to know for sure that the most important time is now, the most important person is the person who is now near you, and the most important act is to do him good. In "***David Copperfield***", the world-famous novel from ***Charles Dickens***, there is no charisma and miracle but the true and heart-rendering story of a child – a child you can find in any city – whose father dies before he was born and who has to suffer the cruelties of his step-father, his exposure to child labor in London, the revenges and poor limits of a child, his dreams and aspirations, his love and expectations. In his well noted poem, "***Abou Ben Adhem***", the poet ***James Henry Leigh Hunt*** does not take us to a complicated world of drama. It simply tells how an angel appears one night before Abou and tells him that he is writing the names of those who love God. Abou was disappointed to know that his name was not in the list but then he gladly said that okay, no problem, but write my name as the one who loves his brethren. The angel came again the next night and told Abou that his name topped the list of those who love God. What can be more simple, more emphatic and more touching? Be simple; that is the best dress for your thought.

2. **Flow:** When we are clear about our idea, we know what to say. This clarity adds momentum to our writing. But if someone is not clear what he has to say, he will have to go – think what to write next. When the power of thought is missing, the writer tends to fill the gap by going zigzagged, by taking longer routes, by showing his 'word-arts' and such things. One of the reasons why legal languages are complicated is this very fact that it is good for the lawyers if people don't understand what they have to say. They say half and they hide half, and this is good for that business. But this is not good for a good writer because it kills the flow of writing and the reader tends to go to sleep. Read whatever you have written. Does it interest you? Is the flow natural? Does your expression touch your own heart? Can you smile, laugh, cry or feel passion by reading your own lines? Could

you notice how fast the time passed by? If your answer to these questions (save the last one) is in 'YES', then it is well done!

3. **Brevity:** It has been rightly said by **Dennis Roth** that "*if it takes a lot of words to say what you have in mind, give it more thought.*" A clear thought is its own ingredient. It needs no hypes and hypocrisies. We must take care that if something can be said in a paragraph, we must not spoil a page for that. Brevity is even more important in modern times when people are fighting against time and have so much to do. Be pert but precise. The basic rule of précis writing is that a passage of 150 words can always be rewritten into its 1/3, i.e., 50 words. So, let it be the standard and try to curtail your writing to make it one-third of what you originally wrote or thought. However, the beauty and fact of the expression should never be compromised. In today's technical writing brevity is very important. It is highly important for writing advertisement, web contents, electronic presentations, catalogues, business proposals, invitations, resume, marketing materials and many things. In all such writings, we are dealing with a reader who wants to know all the features in the shortest possible time and yet the presentation should be appealing enough to attract him to your products or services. It is clear, then, that if you have been able to arrange your 'thoughts' about your products or services (e.g., you know exactly their facts and features), it will not be difficult for you to be 'brief'. To be brief does not mean to be tasteless, unenthusiastic, over-realist and unaesthetic. The main purpose of brevity is to know how to condense our ideas into a power package and present it effectively. The essence of brevity is to learn to trim useless words, superfluous adjectives and roundabout sentences. When you are brief in your writing, you are telling your reader: "*I value your time, I trust in your wisdom and I am sure you are imaginative enough to read between the lines*".

4. **Idealism:** A writer is not a newspaper nor he is a broker in the share-market. People don't need a writer to know "what is". The expanding media is sufficient enough to tell them the '*whatabouts*' of a varied world. A writer is there to tell them "what should be". "What is" serves only as a background for a good writer, a runway for nosing ahead, but the destination is '*what should be*'. Therefore, a writer needs to rise above the 'reporter' status and reach the stage of a

'reformer'. But it should be a natural process; otherwise this world is tired of so many so-called 'reformers'. Thought does not derive its power from 'facts' but 'ideals' – this is now a well-established truth. And this is what great writers always knew. There is a Sanskrit saying – "**Kavirmanishi cha Brahma**" -- which means: "*A poet and a thinker are both Brahma – the Creator*". They just don't live in a world in which they are born but they also create a new world. They are here to serve as our "mirror", and this much is their concern with "what is". By showing us "what is" they also allude to the ugly parts of our realities and inspire us to achieve an ideal status in our personal and collective lives. **Leo Tolstoy** is remembered not because he depicted how snow covered the Siberia but because he told us how to melt the snow of our heart by practicing chastity and living by the principles of love, truth and peace – a thought so penetrating that sparked a personality like Gandhi. People do not know **Jack London** because he built his grand dream house by spending $80,000 (in 1913) – every penny earned by his sweet labour in writing. People know Jack London because his house was burnt to ashes by his enemies, his dreams shattered and he still thought: "*I will still remain the same whose house was put on fire ... Not the one who put the house on fire.*" People remember Kahlil Gibran not because of his reality that he was born poor but because he gave us rich ideals of love in all its profoundness. The most celebrated Hindi novelist, **Munshi Premchand**, had over a hundred reasons to be a 'realist' as his parents died in his teenage; he had to face countless struggles, a wrecked marriage, and life-long financial scarcity. And yet ... all his novels and stories, while sarcastically pointing to "what is" prevailing in our societies, lead us to an ideal world of 'what should be'. The poor boy Hamid prefers to buy a '*chimta*' (tongs) for his grandmother than to spend money on sweets. **Sharat Chandra Chattopadhyaya**, the great Bengali writer most famous for his book "**Devdas**" -- on which more than half a dozen films have been made – lived a hard life till his death in 1938 to cancer, but in all his novels he depicted the ideal beauty and charm of life, of women, of true love, of true human beings. Does it remain to be said that without idealism your thought is lifeless?

Ten Top Tips

1. A good, successful writer is the one who believes, first and foremost, in his or her thoughts.
2. When thoughts are put on the vanguard, right words, flavour, style and other attributes naturally follow.
3. Thought is the first thing to influence human minds.
4. Thought carries two 'place values' for a writer - a generic place value that is related to his personality and a specific place value related to his particular writing.
5. We can make our thought clear by focusing on the subject for a length of time.
6. In the beginning, our thought may be blurred and vague but if we proceed in a spirit of belief, it will be clear later on.
7. At a moment, we must focus only on a small part of our writing, such as 'how to begin it'?
8. Simplicity is the best dress for our thought.
9. When our thought is clear, our writing is fluent.
10. A writer is a creator of an ideal world.

Exercise 7

Match your answers with those given on the ANSWER PAGE. Give yourself 2 marks for each correct answer.

1. **Why is Mahatma Gandhi's "My Experiments with Truth" famous?**
    - A. Because it talks about the cruelties of British rulers.
    - B. Because Mahatma Gandhi made some laboratory tests with truth.
    - C. Because it tells us about non-violence.
    - D. Because of Mahatma Gandhi's sincerity of thought.

2. **What is meant by the 'brand of thought' of a writer?**
    - A. A writer is a market supplier and his writing is like a commodity.
    - B. A writer must be a blind follower of a certain thought.
    - C. A writer should have a firm, time-tested belief summing up his overall personality.
    - D. A writer should never change his ideas whatever happens.

3. **We can develop an insight into how to start writing on a given subject by:**
    - A. Thinking deeply and focusing on that subject for a length of time.
    - B. Going to sleep relaxed and believing that the subconscious mind will find the answer.
    - C. Writing a summary on the postcard.
    - D. Doing nothing but knowing for sure that a dream will guide me.

4. **The statement of George Bernard Shaw that "the drama was quite successful, but the audience failed" reflected his:**
    - A. Self-confidence
    - B. Self-effacement
    - C. Self-criticism
    - D. Vainglory

5. **The touching story of an Afghani nut-seller's love for a small girl is depicted in:**
    - A. Tolstoy's 'Three Questions'
    - B. Tagore's 'Kabuliwala'
    - C. Charles Dickens' 'David Copperfield'
    - D. Sharat Chandra's 'Devdas'

6. **Which attribute of writing is more important nowadays as people are too busy?**
    - A. Simplicity
    - B. Flow
    - C. Brevity
    - D. Idealism

Assignments 7

1. Write a précis of the following paragraph.

   (Model answer given on ANSWER PAGE)

   Had God wanted so, He could have 'forced' mankind to love Him. It was easy for Him! He could have 'forced' human beings to be essentially good and follow Him, but true love does not act that way. Would YOU like that the person whom you love so deeply, should love you back out of a compulsion? Would YOU like a lover who loves you unconsciously, without his or her active choice to love you? Such a 'forced' or 'programmed' lover may be a slave or a robot but not a 'lover' at all. Love is a fellowship … a feeling of being partners … a reciprocal understanding …. an overwhelming emotion of heart between the two … a conscious choice to belong to someone! By giving us FREE WILL, God signed a permanent agreement of love with each one of us – individually! We can choose to love Him, we can also choose not to love Him. He won't compel. Of course, He is craving for our love, waiting like an impatient lover that one day His beloved will return to Him, in His own clandestine ways trying to attract His lover by giving a myriad glimpse of His charming beauty in each atom of the creation, calling him in His tacit language from the valleys of tranquility and mounts of perceptions, beaconing him through simmering stars and shivering blades of grasses, appearing before him in the most cherished face of his beloved to remind him of His aura and aurora, but UNDER NO CONDITION does He 'force' His lover to woo Him. Everyone has to seek that Beloved by himself or herself and this is why we have free will, the power to choose.   [Word Count = 285]

2. Follow the hints and write short stories in about 200 words each. The first one is done for you.

   (A) Born in 1863 in a simple American farmer family……. deep interest in machines since childhood …. in 1896 he created 'Quadricycle' – his first "horseless carriage" ….. it ran on four bicycle tyres ….. worked as an engineer with Thomas Edison …. in 1903, raised $28,000 from 11 investors and created a motor company …. dreamt of making "affordable cars" for all and realized this dream …. Henry Ford.

   This is the story of determination of a simple American child born *in 1863 in a farmer family who, through his dreams, changed the fate of his country and the world. With a keen interest in machines since his early childhood, he foreshadowed his future. As a farmer child, he lived in the company of horses and was familiar with horse-driven carts but he dreamt of making a "horseless carriage". In 1896, he shaped his dream in the form of what he called 'Quadricycle' – because it ran on four bicycle tyres. But this was only the beginning of success for a man who worked as an engineer with a diligent and determined scientist like Thomas Edison. As a poor farmer, he knew the value of money and his ultimate goal was to make motors affordable for all. Setting up a motor company required money and he hadn't enough. But he had something more valuable than money – his determination. By convincing 11 people to invest in his proposed company, he raised $28,000 and eventually realized his long cherished dream of setting up a motor company. This man of iron will was none other but Henry Ford, the founder of Ford Motor Company.*

(B) True story .... a small girl ... ill .... parents sent her to school ..... fell asleep on last bench .... school got over ..... closed for summer vacation ..... class rooms locked .... girl tried to escape ... cried .... lonely area .... died.

(C) 19 July, 2010 ..... train standing on platform ...... small station .... another train from opposite side .... control room staff busy gossiping ... green signal ...... fierce collision ..... 75 died.

(D) Born 28 December 1932 ..... father a school teacher .... at the age of 16 moved to Yemen ..... worked at a gas-filling station ..... came back to India in 1958 with a petty amount and a strong desire .... created billions of rupees by encouraging people's investment .... died in July 2002 ..... voted by the Times of India as "greatest creator of wealth in the century" ..... Dhirubhai Ambani.

(E) A swan .... beautiful golden feathers .... a poor woman with two daughters .... kind swan wanted to help .... gave one golden feather each day .... greedy woman .... one day she caught the swan to take all the feathers .... all feathers changed into ordinary ones .... swan went away never to come back again.

3. Read the brief descriptions of the following products and prepare <u>new</u> (*i.e. do not imitate existing advertisements*) punch lines/slogans

for each one. Show them to your friends/parents/teachers to see how much they appreciate them. <u>The first one is done for you.</u>

- **Godrej furniture** – India-based international company Godrej is a house of established repute, manufacturing a wide range of consumer products. Their furniture range includes state-of-the-art, long lasting, stylish products catering to wide range of usage (home, office, shipyard, hospital, and institutions of various kinds). Godrej furniture reflects remarkable color sense, beauty and space optimization.

    ABIDING BONDS – ENDURING LIFE …. WITH GODREJ FURNITURE!

- **Afghan Herbal Soap** – Afghan herbal soap, an ideal soap for shining hair and glowing skin, comes from the renowned producer of Afghan Snow (skin cream). This nice-looking transparent soap is made of skin-protective and moisturizing herbs and 100% vegetable oils such as Neem, Karanjia, Eucalyptus, Castor, etc. Blending the traditional skincare with modern technology, Afghan herbal soap has a mild and pleasing aroma.

- **Cherry Blossom Shoe Polish** – An internationally reputed company with British heritage and most trusted for its Shoe Care Products. Their collection of shoe polish, shoe wax, shoe care products and shoe maintenance products give you everything you need to protect, nourish, revive and extend the life of your footwear - and to keep your feet feeling and looking great! The company also claims to take special care of environment while making its products.

- **Parker Pens** – Globally renowned Parker pens represent a class of excellence, and to write with a Parker pen is truly a status symbol! Using finest materials and ultramodern technologies in making pens, Parker is proud of its long experience …. since 1888. If you are looking for a pen reflecting style and quality, innovation and durability – Parker is your ultimate goal. There's one for every budget and taste!

- **Barbie Dolls** – Well-known fashion dolls manufactured by the American toy-company Mattel, Inc. Barbie dolls are 'close to reality' and made in finest tuning with the taste and imagination of kids and teenagers. Since 1959, Barbie dolls and toys have kept changing according to the changing times and have included latest mindsets of teenagers. They are so popular that in every second of every day, two Barbie dolls are sold somewhere in the world.

Chapter 8

Be 'Love-intoxicated'

This is love – to fly towards a secret sky,
To cause a hundred veils to fall each moment.

– Rumi

The greatest enemy of a writer's creativity is intoxication, i.e., when he becomes a slave to artificial stimulants such as wine, drugs, LCD, hemp, tobacco and alcohol. Ironically, writers and other creative artists believe that these stimulants are wonderful and increase their inventive powers, open up hidden vistas for incoming of intuitions and 'divine inspirations', telepathic insights and so on. Even young students all over the world are under a similar grip that is spoiling their mind and marring their mental design.

The horrible plight...

The problem of substance abuse among the youth increasingly became so rampant in the last decades that the year of 1995 was dedicated by the United Nations to "***The World Programme of Action for Youth on Drug Abuse***". The findings of the UN were highly disturbing. There are nearly 1 billion young smokers in the world, mostly in developing countries, and this number will be redoubled by 2030. According to school surveys conducted in some European countries in the year 2003, 7-14% of children started smoking by the age of 13, and by the year 2005 nearly 3500 children below the age of 15 were undergoing treatments for severe drug-related diseases. Apart from so many diseases, drugs are also the cause of widespread violence, hooliganism, financial frauds by young children, bullying in schools, etc. In India, over 10 million men, women and children are HIV-positive. Since many drugs, including the popular "*Brown Sugar*", are taken as intravenous injections, AIDS is closely associated with this global problem which increasing in an appalling rate.

A huge cost for a small gain...

There is no doubt that artificial stimulants give a temporary boost to our imagination by inducing our mind to a forced '*alpha*' state, to a coerced sleepiness and suppression of the conscious mind. In the long run, however, they claim for the 'real cost' incurred. All these stimulants are like clever 'money-lenders' who allure people to take liberal loans from them. They give you any amount of money very happily and you are glad because you have an easy flow of 'money' to cater to your present needs. You just can't see the future when you will have to pay the 'interests' by hook or by crook. After badly consuming your mind and giving you 'hallucinations' of so-called 'creative inspirations', after taxing all your brain-cells and damaging your natural power of innovation, a time comes when these intoxicants leave you imperiled, and you have to pay huge interests in the form of cancer, dental problems, bad smell, damaged liver, failing kidneys,0hoarse voice, damages related to nervous system, intestinal bleeding, heart attack, perversion, depression, schizophrenia and hosts of mental, physical, moral, spiritual, and financial incapacities.

It is scientifically accepted that cocaine, opium, marijuana, opiates, other drugs and tobacco products serve as 'stimulus' for the time being, and it is possible that you will be able to write a few good pieces, some great novels, film-scripts, etc., but this is also scientifically proven that you will soon be an 'addict', a diseased person and will not be able to write or imagine anything after a few years. Some people even become highly depressed and commit suicide. Is it necessary to pay such a huge cost for a small gain?

K.L. Saigal: An example of a talent nipped in his bud due to alcohol...

You will be able to see for yourself, in your own surrounding, many such 'talents' who could do something worthwhile and of far abiding value, only if they had refrained from the artificial "mood-makers", as they call them, and had relied on the natural inborn powers of their mind. You must have heard of many great artists who were full of capabilities and ended their life in misery just because of their uncontrolled addiction. They never knew that God gave them an innate and 'unconditional' talent ... and there was no need to rely on artificial stimulants for their vent. Among great artists in their respective times, I know about **Kundal Lal Saigal**, a dazzling meteor of the Indian cinema before Independence. So soulful was his voice that, in that early era of cinema, many people would virtually swoon listening to his songs. He was loved and admired by millions for his great acting. And yet such a loved and valued artist chose to find solace in alcohol than in the intoxicating love of people. He would never go and record a song unless he had consumed alcohol. One famous musician, **Naushad**, requested him to sing for him without the influence of alcohol, and Saigal did so. It is said that he sang much better than he would when he was drunk. So nicely he sang that he hugged Naushad, cried and said: '*How well if I could have found a man like you before*'. But, alas! by that time alcohol had gripped him in its ugly claws and he died a tragic death when he was only 42. Had Saigal shunned alcohol, he could have lived longer and sang more melodies in this coarse world.

What is the role of these intoxicants? Why do writers and creative artists take resort in them? Normally, these intoxicants function by forcefully repressing the conscious mind which is responsible for logic and reasoning, analysis and synthesis. As long as the conscious mind is active, the subconscious mind will remain dormant. And the conscious mind is a decisive mind, a 'realist' mind. It reminds us of our pain and sufferings, realities and limitations. Resorting to drugs, wine, etc., suppresses the '*feelings of reality*' that the conscious mind has. Now, since there is no reasoning, any unexplainable mind-view seems to the person as a 'great, unique experience'. Moreover, several studies have clarified that these intoxicants make the ventral tegmental area (VTA) of the brain hypersensitive. The chemicals – especially dopamine and Serotonin - released from the VTA neurons increase movement, emotional 'highness' and a sense of ecstasy or euphoria. It is this great feeling of delight, inner inspiration and the increased urge for creativity that people, especially writers and artists, enslave themselves to artificial stimulants. But as soon as the intoxicating effect is gone, 'realities' come back. There is no permanent solution, and so the person needs to suppress his conscious mind again, and the cycle goes on. Even in the United Nations' World Youth Report 2005, it has been pointed out that "***the use of drugs, tobacco and alcohol may become a means of escaping from situations that youth often feel powerless to change***". But, no, the power to change the condition will never come from staggering gaits and inebriated minds. It will come by drinking a celestial wine described as follows.

The wine of God...

How encouraging it is to know that God has created a very powerful intoxicant which has no side-effects of any puerile behaviour or psychosis; no hallucinogenic mirages or temporary 'highs'! So sweet is its taste and so rich are its psychedelic experiences that any artificial stimulant cannot stand even as a fraction of its potency. There are no negative aftermaths – only positive control over yourself and as the poet, **Rumi**, described above, it will unveil to you countless wonders of the universe. Like any other intoxicant, this divine intoxicant, too, will fill you with such an ecstasy and emotional upswing that you will cast away the whole world to drink a draught of this celestial nectar. This potent, timeless wine of God is love!

Like drugs and all other artificial stimulants, love also has its chemistry and neurology. How interesting to note that the same neurotransmitters such as dopamine and serotonin are released in the brain when we take intoxicants which are also released when we reflect the feelings of love! Phenyl ethylamine is yet another important *"love chemical"* released from the pituitary gland which elevates the mood and intensifies sensational feelings. Thus the condition of a drug-addict and a lover is almost the same. Both behave out of logic, both have lunacies, both dwell in a 'different' world of their own. But there's a difference – the former is destructing his soul, the latter is uplifting it.

Love is the only creative force of life. God created this universe for only one reason – His love for us. And love is the only multiplying force of the universe – when you spread love, it becomes manifold and reverts to you as a rebounding energy. Love is the binding element of life which promotes harmony and balance. In a state of love, we do not become 'illogical' like a drunken fellow. To use a better word, love makes us 'super logical'. We think beyond normal spheres of reasoning. That's why a mother sacrifices her comforts for her children. Had she been 'logical' like ordinary people, she would have thought of herself first. A warrior loves his country and becomes 'super logical'. He takes every trouble to keep up the pride of his nation. Such a sacrificing soldier cannot be compared to a person under the spell of a drug. It is clear, therefore, that even though the 'chemical' composition of love-addiction and drug-addiction are almost the same, there is a far striking 'spiritual' difference.

Love, in its truest sense, is our love for God – that is the source of all love and the projecting centre of all creativity. Scientists who have deeply studied the human brain, have agreed that human brain seems to be designed in a special way – far different from that of any animal – which enables the mankind to receive divine guidance and inspirations in an automatic way. There is no need to use any artificial stimulant to get these inspirations. For example, studies concerning the brain's activities during prayer and meditation proved a heightened state of consciousness – such a state in which the subconscious mind connects itself to the 'higher realms of wisdom'. Thus, when such conducive and positive ways are available, it makes no sense why one should seek 'creativity' in harmful substances.

Love modeled their lives and creations…

Therefore, anyone desiring to be an excellent writer must stop prematurely killing his or her writing career by giving in to satanic stimulants. The godly wine of love is much better and energizing.

Love is that ambrosia which transformed many ordinary people into all-time immortals. There was an **Ann Rutledge**, loved by a man who became one of the most luminous Presidents of America. He could never forget her impressions and her sad death when she was only 22. Ann's impact on **Abraham Lincoln** was also eternal.

And there was a **Beatrice**, a pretty fairy-like girl of 8 years when a boy of almost her own age saw her first time and was mesmerized. He carried her image in his eyes but it was after several years when Beatrice was 17 and greeted him once smilingly when they met across in a street. That smile became the greatest asset of that love-lit boy. **Dante Alighieri** had no frequent interactions with Beatrice but she became his idol, his ultimate definition of heavenly beauty who, in his renowned poem – **The Divine Comedy** – guided his soul to the loftiness of the paradise. Really, what else than pure love can lead us to the heavens!

Here was a promising poet from Persia serving as a delivery boy in a bakery of Shiraz who once went out to deliver bread and came across an intoxicating damsel – **Shakh-e-Nabat** – whom he immediately made his goddess. So intense was his desire to find Shakh-e-Nabat that he vowed to keep 40 nights' vigil at a sacred tomb as it was believed that whosoever will do that, will be granted his desire. The story goes that one night an angel of God appeared before him and asked him his desire. The beauty of the angel surpassed all beauties of the mortal world, and the man constantly gazed at her, forgetting of everything else. When the angel repeated her question, he forgot to beg for Shakh-e-Nabat. He thought, "*If an angel of God possesses such beauty, how beautiful must God be!*" And suddenly he begged, "*I want God*". This man who was raised to the lofty heights of divine love from the base of mortal love was none other but one of the greatest poets from Persia on whom this beautiful country and the whole world prides – **Hafez**.

Hafez's love intoxicated him to write the loveliest poems of all times and a rich collection of his mystic *ghazals* – **Divan**. Among the Muslims, this is considered a highly sacred book. Another book of another poet is equally respectable for the Hindus. The story is almost the same – transformation of a mortal love to love for God. There was a woman named Ratna whom her husband loved profoundly ... so much so that once **Ratna** went to stay with her parents. The love-intoxicated husband could not bear this temporary separation and rushed overnight to see his wife, not even caring that it was raining heavily and the night was dark. Ratna was ashamed to see her man so infatuated that he did not even care what her parents would think. To a man who might have expected love and acceptance from his wife, the woman said: "*I am but a simple creature of flesh and blood for whom you are displaying so much attachment. How I wish if you were to reflect even a fraction of this love for God!*" The fogs of worldly allusions dispersed and the darkness of ignorance was dispelled. Thus was born a great poet of India – **Tulsidas** – whose book '**Ramcharitamanas**' is worshipped in every Hindu house.

Nature is another lofty expression of God's great attributes and can be so engrossing as to capture the complete attention of a personality who was the Poet Laureate of England from 1843 to 1850. **William Wordsworth's** lovely mother died when he was 8 years and later he also lost his father. Apart from his parents, the person he most loved was his younger sister, Dorothy, but she was also separated from him. All these losses drew Wordsworth close to nature and he became a poet through whom mother nature revealed all her tender love and feelings. Many of his poems are written for **'Lucy'**. It is a question if Lucy was a real girl or an imaginary character but the poet's love for the child seems to be intensely passionate.

Such were these people – transformed by the power of love! From **Hans Christian Anderson** whose love for an opera girl, **Jenny Lind**, spurred him to write passionate stories like *"The Nightingale"* to Voltaire – one of the most influential writers of the French Revolution era – whose cordial partnership with Emilie resulted in valuable intellectual collaboration such as in writing the book *"Elements of the Philosophy of Newton"*, the intoxication of love yielded much more than a goblet of wine could.

Make an idol to worship...

Creation needs a propelling force. You must have a cause to live for, an ideal to aspire for. Without a purpose or motivation, you cannot write well. For different people this motivation can take different forms. One can write to please his or her children or parents, a lovely sister or a dear friend. One can write to create a value for his own personal life. Many writers created themselves just 'out of dust' to prove their individual significance to a society which considered them as worthless. Many writers became great because they wanted to serve a humanitarian purpose and collect money for charities. There are also writers who simply wanted to earn money for their own pleasure and were motivated to write a book purely for their *"show me the money"* impulse. When **Anthony Burgess** wrote the famous *"A Clockwork Orange"* crime-thriller in 1962, he just wanted quick money. When J.K. Rowling started the *"Harry Potter"* series, she was financially pressed and her immediate urge was to uplift her condition. When **Charles Dickens** and his father were walking down a country lane, he was just a small child. On the way, the view of a majestic palatial house drew his attention. The child liked the house so much that he immediately expressed his desire to his father. He replied: *"If you were to work hard, one day this mansion would be yours"*. Charles resolved something in his mind and remembered his father's words. In 1856, several decades had passed since that childhood dream was cherished, when Charles Dickens actually bought that 'mansion'. This is how motivation works!

Create an ideal for yourself, cherish a vision, and enkindle a love. If there is no 'real' love in your life, be like **Pygmalion** – the legendary Greek sculptor – who fell in love with an ivory statue he made, and loved her so intensely that goddess Venus turned that statue into a living woman. When you will create and love your ideal, one day you will see it vibrating with life – as a real sensation! If there is nobody to be your 'living model', to inspire and appreciate your intense longing for a lofty purpose, be like *Eklavya* – the downtrodden character of the *Mahabharata* – and carve out a clay model of your ideal teacher, Drona. One day you will hit the bull's eye.

Starting with simple motivations…

When the child is young, parents and teachers can help him or her in setting motivation points – not only for writing but for any good act. These motivation points could be as simple as giving a chocolate or appreciation when the child has done something good or written a good piece of article, poem or prose, or they can be in the form of giving a wonderful prize, books or novelties.

When you are motivated, you are urged to write something better. Start with simple self-motivations, such as writing a poem for your mother on Mother's Day, compiling a lovely book of quotations to be presented to your father on Father's Day. Write something in the honour of your teacher to surprise him or her on Teacher's Day. Write something in gratitude to God, believing that it will make Him so happy as to bestow you with greater talents. Organize an essay competition in your school and give prizes to the winners. Make an editorial team of children to completely edit their school magazine on their own, with little help from teachers. These small motivations really go a long way. Many poets and writers of 'tomorrow' are born out of their school magazines. It may be exciting for a child to see his or her small write-up published in the school magazine. I, too, had written a poem on Gandhi, for my school magazine and though I forgot the lines I wrote, the delight of one of the earlier writings is still redolent.

Whatever good and great we do in this life is because of our motivation, our love for something or someone. And this love can reveal itself through countless vistas. It is not only love for beauty and appreciation that counts. One can pick up his pen to express the grief of Africa's starving children. One can sharpen his pen to free the suffering women from the callous clutches of iniquitous men. Tears flow down the cheeks of millions; one can use these tears and glooms of hearts to ink of one's pen – like *Evelyn Waugh* – and say:

*Don't laugh at me, I'm well aware
That instead of in the inkwell there
I have dipped my pen in the dusk.*

From an endangered peacock to a flying lark – There are so many things to be 'loved'. Our love for any of these, for a person, for our own self, for promotion of a cause, for expression of a better self – when intense and spontaneous -- activates miraculous creative energies inside us. Is this wonderful creation of God not in itself an example? According to the *Vedas*, God was one, hidden in His single, ancient entity. Then He wanted to be loved and a fire surged in Him – the fire of desire. He said "BE" and the one became many. The obscure became expressed in the nature, in mankind, flora and fauna, in desires of hearts, in illuminations of minds. The same God-pattern works in all areas of creativity … for writers, too!

Ten Top Tips

1. The greatest enemy of a writer's creativity is intoxication.
2. Drugs are the cause of many diseases, violence, hooliganism, financial frauds, and several mental disorders.
3. AIDS and drugs often go hand in hand.
4. Artificial stimulants are only effective for a short time and then they tax us heavily, prematurely killing our imaginativeness.
5. Harmful intoxicants help in releasing in our brain some chemicals which forcefully increase our mental activity level and feelings. This has a negative effect later on.
6. The same chemical and neurological changes take place when we are charged with love – and this is a positive change.
7. Love is that ambrosia which transformed many ordinary people into all-time immortals.
8. Love and motivation is vital for a writer. This can assume any form, such as love for God and nature, for a cause or a mission of life, and so on.
9. Parents and teachers can play a vital role in encouraging children to feel motivated.
10. When motivated, we are urged to write something better. We can start with simple self motivations.

Exercise 8

Match your answers with those given on the ANSWER PAGE. Give yourself 2 marks for each correct answer.

1. **Why is AIDS closely associated with drug abuse?**
    - A. Because drugs are exposed to human blood in laboratories.
    - B. Because many drugs contain HIV virus.
    - C. Because many drugs are taken as I.V. injections.
    - D. Because AIDS and drug abuse are both results of ignorance.

2. **What is dopamine?**
    - A. Brain cells serving as "mood-makers".
    - B. A certain chemical released in our brain.
    - C. A harmful drug made of opium.
    - D. An anti-depressant medicine.

3. **One of the reasons pointed out in the United Nations' World Youth Report 2005 for increasing use of drugs, tobacco and alcohol among youths was:**
    - A. Hormonal changes taking place in the growing youth.
    - B. Distraction from schools and families.
    - C. Escaping from difficult situations of life.
    - D. Seeking delight in new experiments with life.

4. **When do we feel a heightened state of consciousness, a connection to 'higher realms of wisdom'?**
    - A. When a chemical named 'phenyl ethylamine' is released from the pituitary gland.
    - B. Under the hallucinogenic effects of LCD and marijuana.
    - C. During our dreams.
    - D. During prayer and meditation.

5. **Which book was written for quick money?**
    - A. Divine Comedy
    - B. The Good Earth
    - C. A Clockwork Orange
    - D. David Copperfield

6. **Which one of the following women was not associated with any poet or a writer?**
    - A. Ann Rutledge
    - B. Shakh-e-Nabat
    - C. Jenny Lind
    - D. Emilie

Assignments 8

1. Write a short essay (note more than 1000 words) on "Drug Abuse and the Youth" and show to your teacher/parents/friends. Ask them to grade your essay as – **A** (for Excellent), **B** (for Good), and **C** (for Satisfactory).

2. Do you know any famous artist or a person in your neighborhood who is/was highly talented but, unfortunately, given to intoxications. Write a paragraph of some 300 words on him/her.

3. Match the following: (*Check answers on the ANSWER PAGE*)

    (i)   Mary   (a) Abraham Lincoln
    (ii)   Ann Rutledge   (b) Dante Alighieri
    (iii) Beatrice   (c) Eklavya
    (iv)   Shakh-e-Nabat   (d) Shelley
    (v)   Ratnavali   (e) Hans Christian Anderson
    (vi)   Lucy   (f) Hafiz
    (vii) Jenny Lind   (g) Pygmalion
    (viii) Emilie   (h) Tulsidas
    (ix)   Ivory Statue   (i) William Wordsworth
    (x)   Drona   (j) Voltaire

Chapter 9

Words Can Be 'Friends'

*By your words you will be acquitted, and
by your words you will be condemned.*

– Jesus Christ (Matthew 12:36-38)

When you know what you have to say, when your thoughts are clear in your mind, your inner impulse for writing will find the way for suitable words to vent your feelings. Words are the basic units of expression of a thought and, therefore, a good writer must have a good stock of words, and, in addition, he or she must also be able to use them rightly for the reason already clarified by the divine teacher in the above Biblical quotation. The words that you use in your writing reveal your personality in the same way as you dress and your mannerism. The words you choose reflect your core thoughts, as said **Kahlil Gibran**: *"All our words are but crumbs that fall down from the feast of the mind."*

So, before we can choose words, we need to have a lot of words at our command. Is it too difficult? No ... not at all!

Our traditional approach for learning words...

Why don't we have a rich vocabulary? Why does it become so difficult for us to find the right word at the right time? Because our attempts at mastering the words are traditionally wrong. As people might have taught you, you are encouraged to read books, newspapers, etc., and as you go through them words will flow. You will, in most cases, know the meaning of the word automatically by guessing what it means in a particular context. If not, you will immediately turn the pages of a dictionary.

This method is <u>not bad</u> but this is also <u>not good</u>, especially when the reader has a very limited word power. Now, if he has to consult the dictionary every now and then, the flow of reading goes away. The entire life he will just be reading books and learning words and never be able to fully benefit from the 'joy of reading'. For an immature reader, guessing the meaning of a word simply by its context is also not safe, and if once a wrong meaning or spelling is settled in his mind, the mistake will keep repeating.

The traditional method is therefore not very sound. It's like sending a soldier to the battlefield and telling him that bullets would be supplied on spot as per need. Nay, a confident soldier must go to the battlefield with sufficient bullets in his possession and, then, if need be, more bullets would be supplied on spot. The wise course, therefore, is not to rely on learning words by reading books but on learning them beforehand. It does not mean that we have to wait till all the words are learnt and suspend reading till that time. Reading must go hand in hand and is really an important factor in increasing your word power but the joy of reading is not involved only in knowing words. Therefore, we must already have a rich vocabulary at our command so that we don't have to pause on every paragraph just to look into a dictionary.

For every person who is desirous to master the vast resources of words, an important step should be to change his attitude towards dictionary. <u>Stop considering your dictionary just as a reference book, as a 'silent and inactive teacher' whom you consult only in need</u>. Rather, consider your dictionary as a living book and read it as you would read a novel or a story.

Words expand our mental vistas...

Before you start on this journey of exploring words, there's good news for you! It is not necessary to have a vast treasure of words to be a good writer. If you have a normal word power of even 5000 words – all at your command – you are a sure success in writing (and speaking, too!). Even in a book of 500 pages, usually not more than 5000-7000 words are used, repeated throughout. A writer should focus mainly on the 'use of words' than on 'profuse of words'. It is also not necessary that a writer has to showcase his multifarious words to win the hearts of the readers. The writings that have moved millions of hearts in the most effective manner are words of the Prophets and they are very simple. A simple word can often touch hearts where pompous words fail. But, of course, there is also one counterbalance that's highly important: you should not use a certain word so many times that the reader is bored.

In brief, your simplicity of words should come from the depth of your thought and not from your poverty in vocabulary. Knowing that we don't need too many words for a successful writing, does not mean that we have now found an excuse to avoid learning new words. It will be important to know that each word is a concept in itself. Never two words are the same ... even if they carry the same meaning. Even if the 'Sun' means the same as *Apollo or Helios*, and the 'Moon' is the same in meaning as *Luna or Diana*, each of these words convey a different picture, stirs up different feeling, and evokes different thoughts. When we discover more and more words, our aesthetic sense develops, our concepts are widened, our mental images get richer colours and tints, and we are able to capture and reflect more subtle treasures of the mind. Is all this not important for a writer? So ... get ready for this fantastic journey!

Preparing a Word Calendar...

No ... you don't have to cram the whole dictionary. But many words are just like your 'friends' – familiar and pleasing! You like them, they spur your imagination, and they instigate your fancies and feelings. When you will 'read' a dictionary, you will come across many words akin to your personality. For example, if you are a sportsman, words like *'amuse'*, *'frolic'*, *'recreation'*, *'merriment'*, *'athletics'*, etc., will seem like exciting your interest. If you are a spiritually-inclined person, words like *'theism'*, *'deity'*, *'monism'*, *'celestial'*, *'cherub'*, *'halo'*, etc., will seem like touching your soul. If your area of interest is arts, there are many words like *'auditorium'*, *'easel'*, *'spectrum'*, *'tinge'*, *'gallery'*, *'connoisseur'*, etc., that will be pleasing to you. The hint is: start capturing the words that are closer to your liking or, in brief, are "friendly words". To prepare a WORD CALENDAR, follow these steps:

1. First of all, identify some 5-6 areas of your interest, such as: sports, cinema, culture, food, health, etc. so that you know your inclination clearly.

2. Buy a big poster-size cardboard from stationary shop as well as sketch-pens of different colors.

3. Write on the top of the card-board – CALENDAR OF MY FAVOURITE WORDS. Then vertically draw 4-5 well-spaced columns on the card-board to write your words in.

4. Sit with a big, good dictionary and start reading all the words from 'A' to 'Z'. It will take weeks or even months to complete, but as

Words Can Be 'Friends'   111

you go through words, stop by the word you liked. For example, under the alphabet 'A', you found a new word 'argentine' which means 'like silver (color)' and you liked this word. So, note it down in the first column of your card-board. Go on like this.

5. Don't write the words' meanings. Only look the meaning in the dictionary and note down the word using different colored sketch pens. By the time your calendar is completed, you will have already learnt 25-30% words or even more, if your memory is sharp.

6. Hang the calendar in your study room. Look at the words frequently and recall their meanings. If you can't, consult the dictionary. In this way, more than 60-70% words will be ready in your mind with their meanings.

The word calendar method is easy, interesting and ensures maximum success. If one cardboard is full, make another calendar. In a couple of months, you should be able to learn over 5000 words. Make a target to learn 5000 new words in two months or so. If you can do it, writing will be an easy job for you.

CALENDAR OF MY FAVOURITE WORDS

A		B	C	D	E
Abbe	Acerbic		Bossed	Conthus	Earl
Abiotic	Adamant		Bot	Canto	Earmark
Ablaze	Ado		Bouncy	Caravan	Earnest
Abound	Advection		Bowline		Echo
Absinth		Bivouac	Brag	Defection	Eclectic
Absolve		Bizarre	Brand-new	Delation	Effigy
Abstract		Blain	Bray	Demigod	Elysium
Abyss		Blister	Brickbats	Denudation	Emerge
Acacia		Bloom		Dialect	Entwine
Acardiac		Blue mould	Cabala	Diameter	Epopee
Accent		Blue murder	Caber	Diffract	Espy
Acclivity		Boast	Cabobs	Dimple	Eve
Accord		Boggy	Cabre	Ding-dong	Exalt
Accrue		Bone-idle	Cabstand	Dingle	
			Camphor		

SAMPLE OF A WORD CALENDAR

Use of Thesaurus and Encyclopedia...

An Encyclopedia (such as *Encyclopedia Britannica*) gives you detailed information of a word or term. Moreover, to further explore the words, using a Thesaurus (such as, *Roget's Thesaurus*) will be very important. A thesaurus gives us a broad list of 'akin' words but you have to know their 'exact' meaning by looking into the dictionary. For example, a dictionary will tell you the meaning of 'house' as 'a place to live in'. Thesaurus can list several words under the heading *'House'*, e.g. *'Kennel'* (where a dog lives), *'Den'* (where a lion lives), *'Igloo'* (where an Eskimo lives), etc. Thus, you will learn more 'friendly words' of your own 'friendly words' ... in the same manner as we make 'new friends' through our 'existing friends'. Simply speaking, if you know 500 words, you will be able to add some 1500 new words just by using a thesaurus.

The word calendar method can be used for this, too. For example, make another word calendar with the heading – MY THESAURUS WORD CALENDAR. Write "HOUSE" on the calendar in a big, bold letters and write as many 'close words' (such as, shelter, abode, dwelling, stable, cow-shed, burrow, tent, etc.) as possible under this sub-heading 'House'.

Children will surely find the word calendar method quite interesting but elderly people – may have hiccups. This is not a justified attitude. Preparing a word calendar using a cardboard and coloured sketches gives a feeling of doing a project work which enhances learning – and this purpose cannot be achieved by other humdrum methods.

Learning assorted words...

The next step to your campaign for the conquest of words may be noting down words of the same 'sort'. For example:

- Make a list of as many diminutive words as you can -- such as, *'lion – cub, 'duck – duckling', 'cow – calf', 'horse – colt', 'flower – bud', 'dear – darling', 'grain – granule', 'river – rivulet'*, etc.
- Make a list of as many words related to a specific field as you can -- such as, "Army" (*Brigadier, Colonel, cantonment, ammunition, revolt, cannon,* etc.), "Space" (*astronaut, galaxy, constellation,*

cosmos, eclipse, stars, etc.), "Kitchen" (*ladle, spoon, coriander, mint, cauldron, apron, sink,* etc.) and so on.

- Make of list of as many antonyms as you can – such as, *'height – depth', 'generous – parsimonious', 'liberal – conservative', 'accept – refuse',* etc.
- Make a list of group-names (i.e., collective nouns) of people or things – such as, a *swarm* (of flies), a *confluence* (of rivers), a *bunch* (of flowers), a *gang* (of robbers), a *fleet* (of ships), etc.
- Make a list of verbs and their noun forms – such as, *act – action, feel – feeling, ascend – ascension, fall – fall, steer – steering, abide – abode, live – life,* etc.
- Make a list of uncountable nouns – such as, *money, beauty, grace, charm, illness, misery, scarcity, prosperity, power,* etc.

These are only some examples to show you how you can start, but the lists are endless and the only limit is your imagination. Imagine as many areas, groups, specific fields, sequences, etc., in which you can explore words. Your friends and parents can also help you.

Knowing the 'Roots'...

English has its roots in ancient languages such as Latin, Greek, Hebrew, etc. Many words currently used in English have been basically derived from these old languages and even though forms of many words have changed, the 'roots' can still be found in the words itself. A 'root' is generally found in the beginning of a word but they can also be found in the middle or the end. Each 'root' denotes a certain meaning and once we know the meaning of these 'roots', we can easily understand the meaning of the words containing these roots. For example 'act' is a 'root' and it means '*to do*'. Now, in all words formed with this root, 'do' will remain as a central meaning. Example: 'Actor' = the person who '*does*' something, 'Action' = '*doing*' something, 'Activate' or 'Actuate' = cause or inspire to '*do*' something, 'Inactive' = not '*doing*' anything, etc. Take another example: "Graph" is a root word which means '*to write*'. When mankind made a progress, the act of 'writing' also evolved. Now 'writing' does not only mean 'writing with a pen on a paper' but it also means 'to imprint', 'to form the image of', 'to draw' an outline manually or mechanically, etc. With this comprehension, it should be easy to understand the meaning of the following words: '*graphic*' (a picture that is 'drawn'), '*autograph*' (auto = self, graph = writing, i.e. something written by the person himself), '*biography*' (bio = life, graphy = writing, i.e. writing about one's life), '*telegraph*' (a writing from distance), '*lithograph*' (a writing on or with the use of stone), etc. Some important 'roots' are enlisted below but there are so many 'roots' and you must discern them when you come across many words sounding almost the same.

> Acri (sour) – example: acrid; Aero (relate with air) – example: aerodrome; Agri/Agro (related with soil) – example: agriculture; Ante (before) – example: antedate; Aqua (water) – example: aqueous; Aster (star) – example: astronaut; Auto (self) – example: autobiography; Bene (good) – example: benevolent; Biblio (book) – example: bibliography; Ceed/Cede (go forward) – example: proceed; Circum (around) – example: circular; Contra (against) – example: contradict; Dec (ten) – example: decade; Dem (people) – example: democracy; Fore (before) – example: foreword; Hetero (not similar) – example: heterogeneous; Homo (similar) – example: homogeneous; Hydr (water) – example: dehydration; Infra (under) – example: infrastructure; Ism (belief) – example: Socialism; Loco (place) – example: localization; Micro (small) – example: microwave; Multi (many) – example: multitasking; Neo (new) – example: neolithic; Oct (eight) – example: octogenarian; Omni (all) – example: Omnipotent; Phobia (fear) – example: hydrophobia; Port (carry) – example: transport; Post (after) – example: post-dated; Semi (half) – example: semifinal; Sept (seven), example: septuagenarian; Super (above/over) – example: superior; Tri (three) – example: triennial; Uni (one) – example: uniform.

Crosswords...

Another useful and mind-stretching method for enhancing your word power is to complete crossword puzzles. Almost all leading newspapers have regular crossword for their readers and you should make a habit to solve them on daily basis. In addition, you can make your own crossword puzzles for your friends and your friends can make for you. This will be mutually useful and very interesting.

A typical crossword, as illustrated here, is made up of a big block with a number of squares to give clue for words horizontally and vertically. The squares which are not used are shaded dark. Try to solve this Crossword puzzle and match your answers with the ones provided on the Answer Page in the end.

A TYPICAL CROSSWORD PUZZLE

Hints:

TOP TO BOTTOM

2. The yellow of the egg

3. Loss of sleep

4. To realize

8. A baby cat

9. A pet bird

10. A kind of sea-food, shell

11. A kind of yellow fossil resin

LEFT TO RIGHT

1. Beauty, grandeur

5. Light, narrow boat

6. An ancient world language/civilization
7. Snarl, bark
8. An intense desire to steal
12. A curved point
13. Clean
14. A type of bird, ~ redbreast.

Learn new words quickly...

A small notebook should always be ready with you to jot down any new word or phrase you come across. If a dictionary is around, look for the meaning right now. Fostering the habit of ignoring new words, not being alert and active enough to learn them as soon as they appear, will make you more and more careless as you grow. Every treasure is gathered bit by bit, so are words. If you learn even 5 new words daily (is it difficult?) You will have learnt more than 1800 words in a year. How rewarding and yet how easy!

Ten Top Tips

1. Words are the basic units of expression of a thought.
2. Our words reveal our personality.
3. It is not bad to learn new words whilst reading but to preserve the 'joy of reading' we must already have a rich word power.
4. Let's consider our dictionary as a living book and read it as we would a novel or a story.
5. A writer needs to pay more focus on the use of words than on profuse of words.
6. Our simplicity of words should come from the depth of our thought and not from our poverty in vocabulary.
7. Each word is a concept in itself. Never two words are the same ... even if they carry the same meaning.
8. There are many fun-filled and effective ways to enrich our vocabulary. Preparing a Word Calendar, use of a thesaurus, solving crossword puzzles are some of these methods.
9. The more words we learn, the more we expand our mind and our ability to express.
10. We must develop the habit of instantly learning any new word we find.

Exercise 9

Match your answers with those given on the ANSWER PAGE. Give yourself 2 marks for each correct answer.

1. **According to the Bible, why should we be cautious of using our words?**
     A. Because words are costly.
     B. Because there are some indirect taxes on our words.
     C. Because our words can have both a good and a bad consequence.
     D. Because each word is an utterance of God.

2. **What does Kahlil Gibran mean by this statement: "All our words are but crumbs that fall down from the feast of the mind."**
     A. All words are already used words.
     B. There is no originality in any word.
     C. Our words reflect our mental properties.
     D. Words are first created in mind.

3. **Why is a dictionary referred to as a 'silent and inactive teacher' in this chapter?**
     A. Because it teaches us about words without making any noise.
     B. Because we use dictionary merely as an occasional reference book.
     C. Clearly because a dictionary is not like a human teacher.
     D. Because dictionaries help us only when we seek their help.

4. **'Each word is a concept in itself' – What does it mean?**
     A. Each word used by a writer reflects his mental concept.
     B. Each word refers to a different meaning.
     C. Each word is equally weighty and mind-moving.
     D. Each word produces a different picture, a different feeling.

5. **What is the use of a Thesaurus?**
     A. Nothing special, it's just a broad dictionary.
     B. It gives us a broad list of related words.
     C. It explains words within a sentence.
     D. It's a dictionary of idioms and proverbs.

6. **The words 'import' and 'export' have a common root, i.e. 'port', which means:**
     A. To carry   B. To lead
     C. To result   D. To communicate

Assignments 9

1. Choose your favourite areas and write at least two words suitable for each area. <u>The first one is done for you,</u> as an example.

   A. CINEMA -- Cinematography, screenplay
   B.
   C.
   D.
   E.
   F.

2. Match the words in Column A with suitable words in Column B. Notice how the two words are closely associated. (Check answers on the ANSWER PAGE)

   Example: (i) Feather = (e) Light

Column A	Column B
(i) Feather	(a) Book
(ii) Leather	(b) Majesty
(iii) Power	(c) Gush
(iv) Sarcasm	(d) Protection
(v) Ruthless	(e) Light
(vi) Dominant	(f) fervor
(vii) Shelter	(g) Shining
(viii) Palace	(h) Thought
(ix) Emotion	(i) Murder
(x) Water	(j) Comment
(xi) Preamble	(h) Control

3. Write the diminutives of the following. (***Check answers on the ANSWER PAGE***) **Example:** Lion – Cub

   (i) Ass: _____
   (ii) Cat: _____
   (iii) Deer: _____
   (iv) Dog: _____
   (v) Frog: _____
   (vi) Goat: _____
   (vii) Hare: _____

(viii)	Horse:	_____
(ix)	Lion:	_____
(x)	Sheep:	_____
(xi)	Swan:	_____

4. Find the following words in an Encyclopedia (such as Encyclopedia Britannica) and write down in your own words short details about them.

    A. Eskimo
    B. Brasília
    C. Orchid
    D. Holocaust
    E. Opera

5. Make a list of things you can easily find near a super market or a mall.

6. Make a Crossword for your friend/brother or sister in which you will hide names of historical characters (e.g. Alexander) and/or scientists (e.g. Newton).

Chapter 10

Infusing Life into Your Language

*Beauty is truth, truth beauty, that is all ye
know on earth, and all ye need to know.*

– John Keats

Generally speaking, what is your definition of life and where does it 'live' in a living thing? Everything is intact even in a dead body – all the body parts remain in their proper places – and yet there is no '*life*'. And what is beauty? Does beauty come in a certain colour? If yes, then all other colours have no charm. Is beauty in a certain state or condition, such as height, complexion of skin, black or brown eyes, wide or narrow brow or chin, a typical stature or built? If yes, then all such standard conditions will become ideal definition for beauty and the rest will be worthless.

Write from your heart...

Life is an 'unseen' force which can be 'felt' in totality of a being. Beauty is an 'invisible' property but which can be appreciated in coordinated proportion of everything in a person or an object. This is how all spiritual aspects can be defined – they cannot be seen superficially but can surely be felt 'inside'.

One can write very well and his writing can contain a number of good factors, such as thoughtfulness, precious ideas, expert presentation, carefully selected words, well-balanced structures, an error-free spell-check, etc., and yet the reader may find no interest in reading a paragraph of his writing. So what is missing? Where is the 'life' gone?

Life, as we understand, was infused out of love by the Great Being. There can be no other stuff, therefore, to create life. When you write something from your heart, it assumes life – no special effort is to be made. When you write something merely from your mind, it drains life. Feel it from your heart, whatever it is, and write. It is a good thing to note that love for writing can be fostered and all the previous chapters are attempted to generate this love in every promising writer's heart.

See things in their totality ...

The Sanskrit word for 'Literature' is *'Sahitya'* and it means 'totality', it also means 'inclusiveness' (*Sahitasya Bhav: ya: sa: sahityam*). Life is not found in nostrils and lungs, in blood circulation and metabolism, and not even in legs, bosoms, ears and hands. All these things express life by combining together, working together, coordinating together.

As is in life, so in literature. When we try to see things and present them in their maximum totality and coherence, we are able to infuse life into our language. Clearly speaking, it means looking into things a bit more deeply than an average person, feeling about them more intensively and viewing them from broader perspectives. *"There is a beggar"*, when this is said to an average person, he would simply cast a glance on the poor beggar, toss a coin and go away. This is his perspective. But if one has to write a poem on that beggar, he is expected to think in a more reflective manner and express something like this:

> *See that skeletal figure!*
> *Tramping with a bamboo-stick in his hand,*
> *Stretching a torn, ragged bag for a handful of rice,*
> *To douse his hunger;*
> *At times he is partaking of wasted food by the roadside*
> *While dogs are competing with him,*
> *To snatch away even those crumbs.*
>
> (Adapted from a Hindi poem of Suryakant Tripathi 'Nirala')

If a child's attention is drawn towards a cat, he will merely look at the poor feline creature, imitate a 'mew' and laugh away, but if the same boy has to write an essay on 'the cat', he cannot bypass the great features of the Tiger's Aunt.

Portray it with your pen...

Life is a moving, dynamic truth. There is no life in stillness and dullness. This being the definition of life let your writing be moving and dynamic, too. An immortal artist like Picasso and Michael Angelo does his best to use the most real tints to draw the most truthful bends and curves, and hint the minutest shades to portray the life-size picture of their heart. We all know the famous story of a king who held a drawing contest to reward the best artist. On the canvas, they had to make 'real-looking' fruits. When all the artists finished their drawings, the king let loose a number of frugivorous birds. All the birds pecked at a particular picture showing grapes and mangoes, strawberries and peas. *"That's the best drawing"*, declared the king because it had the closest resemblance with truth. It looked so real!

Make your pen such a mighty brush of life! Depict things as real as you can. Try to bring every shade, every line, every tint of the various moods of life – its pains and its pleasures. Try to bring that smell, music, rhythm, charm, and ambience which encircle the real object you are writing about. This quality is important for all writers but even more important for news reporters reporting from the actual sight of the scene (such as, a war), for commentators writing about an exciting match, and for film script-writers introducing scenes into the movie.

For example, a war is waged between two countries and you are reporting from the war-front. Instead of sending a normal account as the following,

> ABZN News Reporter. TNT Border. *The situation seems to be extremely tense as the two belligerent countries have declared internal emergency and are exhausting their full resources to fuelling the flame of the catastrophic war. Deadliest bombs are being used to destroy the enemy's posts, fighter planes are crying havoc and the streets are full of giant tanks. Civil life has come to a standstill on both sides of the border as people have to live under incessant curfews and black-outs. Children – afraid and insecure – are experiencing the worst mental trauma of their life. Cloistered in their houses, as schools are completely suspended, they look out of the windows hoping that one morning the sun will be clearer and they can go out to play as the streets will be vacated by the green uniforms. The UN intervention is now of a vital importance.....*

You may wish to send a livelier account like this which gives more picture effect:

> ABZN News Reporter. TNT Border. *The air is agog with hovering war-planes and giant tanks rustling and screeching on roads. 'Boom!' and flames of fire rose several meters high exploding the*

> *camouflaged military bases. No, this is not the shooting of one of those 'Terminator' films of Hollywood but a real tragedy being faced by the people of the two belligerent countries. Shops and recreations centers are no longer open, evenings are no longer vibrant with merry-making girls and boys. Apprehending every moment a new horror, people live confined in their homes. There is no light of hope in their 'black-out' nights nor there is a sunny morning for yesterday's chirping children going to school but now looking with their blank eyes their joyful delights trampled under the heavy boots of the green army. When will the ice melt? Only the United Nations can save these shattering dreams ....*

Or, you are writing a film story, introducing a night scene like this:

> *It is a wonderful moon-lit winter night. The sky is clear except for some white clouds floating here and there, hiding the moon, and the moon reappearing again and again. Its magical light falls on the big lake, and the lake looks so beautiful and romantic. Gentle wind is blowing and small ripples rise and fall in the lake...*

Perhaps it would be better to present a pen-sketch and embodiment that adds more life to the above scenario:

> The pitch-dark night is strewn with golden threads of a charming moonlight. In its full youth, the moon is swimming across the width of the sky, playing hide-and-seek behind the snow-white clouds and shedding her beaming smile on the gently rippling waves of the beautiful lake – an eternal romance in the shivering windy night.

Shun negativism...

Life is a positive energy. It has no place for negative forces. Everything negative contains its own 'death virus' in it while everything positive has a latent seed of life eternal. Keeping this universal spiritual law in mind, the symptom of a life-reflective writing should also be found in its positive thrust. No matter you are writing a piece of news, an ad campaign or a big treatise on *'The Changing Paradigms of the Youth Lifestyles'*, shun negativism. Time has gone when people were so foolish that they believed in *'Neighbour's Envy and Owner's Pride'* concepts. Even a child of the new era clearly knows that we are living in a harmonious world where lingering envies of the neighbour cannot guarantee anyone's abiding pride. Time has gone when reckless criticism, piling the dust of the neighbor's door to prove his untidiness was supposed to be 'bravery' in so-called yellow journalism. Excessive negative curiosity in other's life has taken away many innocent lives like Princess Diana and people of an enlightened generation hate such 'killer' journalists and writers holding their cameras and pens in the name of 'searching the truth.' In this new epoch, when science has clearly proved the all-pervading presence of God element, such negative writers who write 'satanic verses' to bring down a Prophet and others who unhealthily relate the Christ with a Mary Magdalene are no more respected than viewed as news mongers.

Never in the whole history of civilization did a writer become great and popular by focusing on negative aspects of life. Some created a six month sensation and passed away. Life is basically beautiful but if we want to focus on ugly things they are also there. We have to choose on what to focus.

Being positive does not mean being an escapist. It does not prevent a writer from telling about the dark sides of a picture, but it must be borne in mind that revealing those dark sides should add impetus to exploring brighter sides of life. Write about a scandal to reveal the real face of a rotten system and not to glorify the people who are involved. Don't give a report about a politician sunk in corruption and in the same newspaper show he is seated at ease in his palatial home. What's your message? Is it that everybody should be involved in corruption and then buy a mansion and live such a glorious life? Your intention must be clear if you are surfacing the fraudulent schemes to make people aware of their detrimental impacts, or just to sell a few more hundred copies of your newspaper!

Use the negative aspects only to reflect the beauty of positive powers of life, in the same way as a photographer treats the negative in a dark room just to bring out a beautiful positive photograph. Use the character of a Shylock to eulogize kind-hearted Antonio or Portia, and not to teach the hidden tactics of procuring money by exploiting people. This is the method applied by all great authors, including those of wonderful epics like the *Ramayana, the Mahabharata, the Iliad,* and *the Odyssey* – all the timeless stories telling us about the victory of virtue over the vice.

Weave your writing with the positive threads of love and cooperation, appreciation and sympathy, hope and grandeur, truth and morale and you will know that life in writing comes from healthy nutrients and not from the deadly poisons of competitiveness, hatred, materialism, envies, calumnies, negative propaganda and exploitation of people's minds.

Novelty...

Life is new, so should be your writing. Pick up a new theme that others have failed to select for themselves. Every moment countless stories are revealing, numberless new flashes of knowledge beaconing, and unlimited mysteries of the universe opening up. Since thousands of years the apples are falling straight on the earth but a Newton watches and discovers a new truth. You can also be a **Newton** by keeping your eyes wide open to notice even the simplest phenomena of this magnificent creation of God. A writer does not see only through his or her mortal eyes but also inner eyes. He or she does not listen to the call of God only through physical ears but also internal ears of intuition. Helen Keller was both deaf and blind but she proved to be an eminent speaker, a superb author. **Beethoven's** physical ears were unable to hear but his soul could listen to the most tuneful notes of the Unseen. **Homer** was born blind and so was "*The Sun of Hindi Poetry*", **Surdas**, and yet their literary pieces are so full of novel images, freshest similes, unthinkable depth, intricate description of human traits, and they reflect a keen 'inner' observation of the subtlest phenomena of the nature.

Adopt a new style. Be like **Walt Whitman**. When he compiled "**Leaves of Grass**" using a new poetic style, all publishers refused to publish his work, but he believed in himself and went on. If you feel you have something new to say, say. Every writer has to be sincere to himself or herself first. Refuse to follow the beaten track. Declare, as did **Berley**: "*I will find my own way and if I can't, I will make a new one.*"

Say something new, in a new way. Sing a new song, far more melodious than before. Concoct new spectrum of colours, far brighter than before. Give a new idea and let this journey of newness be so engrossing for you that every time there is a new flavour in your writing.

A promising writer must be progressive. Tomorrow he must be far ahead from where he is today. He must learn every moment, must grow every second. Read new books – even if you are 95 years old, even if you are a world-class writer. Keep on thinking and meditating, finding something novel to write about, to create. The life of a river is vested in its flow; the death of a pond is inherent in its stillness.

Strong characters/strong points...

If you are a fiction writer, you are the creator of a world of varied personalities. A writer is '*Brahma*' – the Creator – in this very sense that he brings out a new sparkling world – a world of its own colour, aroma, atmosphere, movement, life, and characters. The more superb your creation of this 'world', the better '*Brahma*' you are.

An artist invests himself in his art. A mother invests herself in her child. A candle invests itself in creating light. A true artist is lost in his art; a true mother has lost her personal desires in moulding her child. A candle is learnt by illumining a darksome world. So you must be in creating your characters. Give birth to characters higher than you ... such higher characters that those who loved you should love your character more than you. As an actor's success depends on how much appreciation he won for his role, as a villain's success is measured in the amount of abuses and curses heaped upon him by the audience, a writer's success is measured in terms of the great or feeble characters he or she has begotten. People may forget you but never forget your creation. **Oscar Wilde** may linger or not, his creation like **Dorian Gray** will leave his imprint on people's mind as someone whose inner trends created a mark on his face – a symbolic character reminding us that what we are inside so we are without. Ask a child, perhaps he does not know **Jonathan Swift** but he is very familiar with **Gulliver** and his travels to Lilliput where all were tiny creatures and then to Brobdingnag where the case was just the opposite. Children, likewise, may not be too familiar with **Rudyard Kipling** but they already have a great affection for his character, the little **Mowgli**, the superhuman character raised by wild wolves. **J.K. Rowling** may be known to intellectuals only and not to those tiny citizens who stick so closely to the TV to watch **Harry Potter**. Perhaps Lewis Carroll is no more popular than the pretty ***Alice in the Wonderland***, and the revolutionary ***Scarlet Pimpernel's*** stature grew higher than its creator **Baroness Orczy**. **George Eliot** was great but even greater is her character **Silas Marner**. Who can forget that falsely accused pious weaver spending his time away from a disenchanting society he lived in and was falsely accused of stealing money? Deceived by his own friend and rejected by the woman he loved, Silas Marner leaves the city to bring tears in our eyes. **Robin Hood** and **James bond** are so popular that nobody believes they are 'imaginary' characters. The entire world of Shakespeare is woven around immortal and versatile characters like **Hamlet, Othello, Portia, Polonius, Lysander, Macbeth,** and so on.

Create timeless characters to create timeless stories. You might be thinking: what elements make a great character? The answer can be found by you. If you will think about some of the characters mentioned above you will know a vital fact – these immortal characters were a pleasing blend of dream and reality. Nobody believes in a character if it is totally unreal, and nobody loves a character if it is as ordinary as you and me. The 'mantra' is: make something out of life but greater than life.

And if you are not writing a fiction, your characters are in the form of your thought, in the shape of the points you want to emphasize. You assume the role of a powerful pleader who brings the best of his arguments, the surest of his proofs, the most indisputable of his logics to defend what he wants to defend and refute what he wants to refute. Potent and powerful details, authentic information, prudent analysis and appealing presentation in a non-fiction work assume the same place as living and vibrant characters in an imaginary story.

Use of figurative language...

Since literature is an art of 'all-inclusiveness', a vibrant writing is that which is capable of correlating things together. When things are thus correlated, not only does the beauty of expression increase but also its comprehensibility. Saying that *'Don is a dull man'* does not draw a picture fuller than this: *'Don is as dull as a donkey'*. Therefore, one of the important life elements of powerful writing is the writer's ability to express his thoughts not just as simple and dull statements but also as cohesive and beautiful statements. Such statements are known as 'figurative' statements because by the very way of their expression they create a 'figure' or a 'picture' that adds life to the language.

The greatest writers have been those who had the ability to correlate different aspects of life together by using figurative language. A figurative language has many characteristics, some of them being: similes, idiomatic expressions, metaphors, allegories, personification or embodiment, etc. Even though all these characteristics slightly vary in nature, basically they are all 'co-relations'. Similes are especially very popular. Kalidas has been an incomparable Sanskrit poet and his most praiseworthy attribute is summarized in this proverb about him – "UPAMA KALIDASASYA", i.e. Kalidas was matchless in using the similes. His entire poetry is enriched with 'comparisons' like *'the peacock spreading its tail feathers and reminding him of his wife's hair adorned with flowers of different kinds', 'the color of her lips like that of a morning sun', 'the silver clouds kissing the black boulders of mountains'* and so many other excellent similes.

"*Death lies on her like an untimely frost*", is a beautiful expression of William Shakespeare to give 'death' a figure of a miserable shadow, a mystic shroud. William Shakespeare was a marvelous master in observing human nature:

> Blow, *blow, thou winter wind,*
> *Thou art not so unkind*
> *As man's ingratitude ..*

Note: How ironically he correlates the bitterness of the winter wind with even more bitter experience that we have when we meet an ungrateful man. Thus the quality of nature has been correlated with the quality of man.

When **Tulsidas** vents: "*O Tears of my eyes! Remain intact in the corner of the eyes itself, like gold intact with a miser man*" (*Lochan jal rahu lochan kona / Jaise param kripan kar sona*), observe what a deep *correlation* is drawn between a simple act of 'not *letting the priceless tears flow*' and '*how a miser man does not let his gold loose*'.

Expressions like "*O my love is like a red, red rose*" (**Robert Burns**) and "*When the evening is spread out against the sky like a patient etherized upon a table*" (**T.S. Eliot**) will always be striking for their inherent beauty.

All fordone and forgot;
And like clouds in the height of the sky,
Our hearts stood still in the hush
Of an age gone by.

What a befitting and serene relationship has the poet, **Walter De La Mare**, drawn between '*clouds in the height of the sky*' and the '*hearts stood still in the hush of an age gone by*'!

All these great poets and authors have taught us that everything in life is, in some way, closely inter-related with each other and it is the versatility of a writer how he or she attributes this correlation.

Equally important is using, in a moderate degree (and not too much), idiomatic and proverbial expressions as they, too, help in delivering a more picturesque message. Thus, a simple statement like "*please wait and don't always be in a hurry; it takes time in completion of a viable work...*" can be more suitably delivered in this way: "*please wait and make no haste; Rome was not built in a day...*".

Like any art of expression, the uses of similes and idiomatic expressions will greatly depend on how well you observe and how intense is your power of imagination.

Ten Top Tips

1. The "life" in our writing comes only when we write it from our heart.
2. The Sanskrit word for 'Literature' is 'Sahitya' and it means 'totality' and 'inclusiveness'.
3. When we try to see things and present them in their maximum totality and coherence, we are able to infuse life in our language.
4. Make your pen a mighty brush of life; depict things as real as you can.
5. Try to bring that smell, music, rhythm, charm, and ambience which encircle the real object you are writing about.
6. Don't focus your writing on negative aspects of things. Negative writing has a short life.
7. Use the negative aspects only to reflect the beauty of positive powers of life.
8. Life is new, so should be your writing. Adopt a new style. Say something new, in a new way.
9. People may forget you but never your creation. Create timeless characters to create timeless stories.
10. The greatest writers have been those who had the ability to correlate different aspects of life together by using a figurative language.

Exercise 10

Match your answers with those given on the ANSWER PAGE. Give yourself 2 marks for each correct answer.

1. **We can say that there is 'life' in someone's writing when:**
    - A. the reader is interested in reading that writing.
    - B. the wiring is presented in audio-visual format.
    - C. the writer has used figurative language.
    - D. there are no errors in the language.

2. **We are able to infuse life in our language when:**
    - A. we use enough brains and logic.
    - B. we try to be plain and straightforward.
    - C. we try to include totality and coherence.
    - D. we imitate a famous writer.

3. **What is a pen-sketch?**
    - A. A drawing made with the use of ink.
    - B. An outline or contour of an object.
    - C. A true and living depiction of something in writing.
    - D. Using different colors of ink to draw an attractive picture.

4. **How did Princess Diana die on 31 August, 1997?**
    - A. In a car accident while being chased by paparazzi.
    - B. In a plane crash with her fiancé Dodi Fayed.
    - C. Due to a royal conspiracy at the behest of Prince Charles.
    - D. During a TV interview.

5. **Which one of the following is NOT a character created by Shakespeare?**
    - A. Polonius
    - B. Shylock
    - C. Hamlet
    - D. Silas Marner

6. **Potent and powerful details, authentic information, prudent analysis and appealing presentation in a .... work assume the same place as living and vibrant characters do in an .... story.**
    - A. Research, artistic
    - B. Fiction, illusive
    - C. Literary, imaginary
    - D. Non-fiction, imaginary

Assignments 10

1. Draw a pen-sketch of the following in not more than 200 words. The first one is done for you as a model.

    - The traffic in my town –

    I live in a small city with a population of some 500,000. Just imagine a beautiful city surrounded by lush-green hills all around with a majestic fort stretching afar. It was once a small kingly estate in the British time with tall archaic buildings. Now it's developed into a modern city. Population is expanding but roads are still the same 10-meter wide pathways. In peak hours, that is time when children go to and come from their schools and men and women rush to and from their offices, even an ant cannot pass through the streets. The number of two-wheelers and four-wheelers is increasing and their smokes are now suffocating the people of this 'Fortified City'. A poor traffic constable with a small baton in his hands is running to get hold of the rule-breakers and they are guffawing at him on speeding motorbikes. Another one is driving and talking on mobile and police can do nothing. There is no left or right. You are walking on your side and suddenly a screeching car can just pass half-touching you. There are dangerous overtakings and only God can save your life. Want to come to my town for a visit?

    - My best teacher
    - A funny character I like
    - My jolly friend ……….. (name your friend)

2. Introduce a horror scene, depicting an abandoned church or an old building and a dark midnight.

3. You want an artist to draw a painting of your mother but you don't have her photograph. All you can do is to give the artist a description of your mother in words so that the artist can portray her image based on his own imagination. Write a perfect description suggesting the artist about the nature, built, facial expressions and other useful details about your mother.

4. Someone has written an application to the Mayor of a City Council. As you can see, it sounds bitterly negative. Edit the application to eliminate negativity and give it a positive touch. (***Model answer given on ANSWER PAGE***)

To,

Joseph Carlos
Mayor
The City Council of Aidenburgh

Dear Mr. Carlos,

I feel concerned to let you know the condition of our area which has virtually become a stinking hell for all the residents. For over a week the garbage collectors have not attended the area. As a result, the dustbins are lying in front of houses with nobody to lift them up. The intermittent rain has worsened the condition and the waste materials are not only stinking badly but also contaminating drinking water sources.

Earlier this year, when we had voted for your Green Party, we had set high hopes on you all but now we feel we have been befooled and are totally neglected when it comes to providing us essential services. Your officers and contractors are getting over a thousand dollar per month for cleanliness services and still people have to suffer all this inconvenience.

I hope you will take some immediate steps to lift up the garbage so that we are not compelled to think about some serious measures like a public protest.

Yours faithfully,

John Groan
Edmonton Cross

5. Match these famous characters with their writers:
   (*Check answers on the ANSWER PAGE*)

   Characters   **Writers**
   (i)   Macbeth   (a) Boris Pasternak
   (ii)   Silas Marner   (b) W. M. Thackeray
   (iii) Mowgli   (c) Miguel de Cervantes
   (iv)   Gulliver   (d) George Eliot
   (v)   Anna Kerenina   (e) William Wordsworth
   (vi)   Dr. Zhivago   (f) Kalidas
   (vii) Beatrix   (g) William Shakespeare
   (viii) Dushyanta   (h) Rudyard Kipling
   (ix)   Lucy   (i) Leo Tolstoy
   (x)   Don Quixote   (j) Jonathan Swift

Chapter 11

The Magic of 'AIDACADEBRA'

> *A scrupulous writer, in every sentence that he writes, will ask himself at least four questions, thus: 1. What am I trying to say? 2. What words will express it? 3. What image or idiom will make it clearer? 4. Is this image fresh enough to have an effect?*
>
> *– George Orwell*

This 11th and last chapter is designated to focus on 11 "key letters" that contain all the vital elements of a successful and effective writing. The chapter concludes the main ideas contained in the previous chapters, and provides the students a more concrete and memorable formula that is easy to understand and serves as a check-point for everyone.

Remember this 11-lettered formula of AIDACADEBRA while writing and even after you've completed your work, to check if everything is in its place.

The first four letters of this magic formula for writers – AIDA – is already popular in the advertisement world but they relate it with all effective writing. So here is how each letter of this magic formula stands for you, an aspiring writer.

A = Attention

Your writing always has a target. You are writing for someone. Even if you are an amateur writer, you are writing for your own delight. So the target is still there – you, yourself. And you have already learnt that everything is correlated. So what delights you is sure to delight many others. Well, so remember that since your writing is for a targeted reader, your first duty is to draw the attention of your reader. To accomplish this, you have to follow the three steps:

1. THINK who your readers are. Their age, gender, location, background, culture, educational level, beliefs – consider everything.

2. DECIDE what type of language (easy or high level), style and tone (humorous or scholarly, etc.) should be used.

3. IMAGINE how you can invite them into the subject in the first sentence or first paragraph. What type of beginning will appeal them?

For example, you are writing a fairy tale. Naturally, your targeted readers are children. The type of language must be easy, colloquial and fun-filled. What will grab their attention is likely to be the charm and beauty of the fairy, her kind-heartedness and her power to create miracles, etc. Now, each writer can think of his or her own way of starting the story. If the story is being written for a TV show, for example, the approach may be more visual than narrative. If the story is being written to be relayed on radio or published in print media, a beautiful narration to start the story will be important. One can start with a question, like: *"Children, have you ever met a fairy whose touch would cause the flowers bloom and rivers warble? Gazalla was such a mesmerizing fairy."* Another writer can start by giving a visual impact: *"It is a dark, deep night. There is silence everywhere and cool breeze is blowing while the sky is teeming with twinkling stars. And ... oh! From where did a sweet fragrance come? All the sleeping flowers bloomed and smiled, birds hustled out of their nests. Gazalla, the pretty fairy of Dreamland is alighting from the sky...."* Yet another writer can prefer to choose a spell-binding traditional narrative style: *"Long ago, in the enchanted forest of Dreamland, there lived a blue-eyed, rosy-cheeked fairy named Gazalla. So beautiful and gracious was she and so radiant was her face that flowers would bloom at night seeing her and birds would start chirping in their nests that, lo! it dawned."*

Be your original self and write in your own way.

I = Interest

It is good that you have focused on your targeted readers, used the exact type of language, style and form that is suitable for them, and have started your writing in such a way as to draw their attention. Now, attention once drawn does not guarantee that attention will continue. You have to ensure that the readers' attention is sustained throughout your writing. You have to keep your readers <u>interested</u>. This is a task more challenging than drawing their attention. This is the art of maintaining the momentum. Some tips that can be useful to win the interest of your reader are as follows:

1. Take care of paragraphing. Nobody wants to read long, boring passages. If appropriate, use sub-captions in betweens.
2. Use bullets when giving long lists, points, etc.

3. Avoid monotony in writing. Keep on changing styles, descriptions, incidents, scenes, characters, etc., to give a shade of variety. Introduce short stories, allegories, parables, etc. in betweens, if suitable.

4. Maintain the flow of your writing by putting your 'heart' in each paragraph. Let no paragraph be a dull paragraph.

5. If appropriate, make your writing interactive, i.e. ask direct questions to readers; keep them involved in the subject. Feel their presence throughout your writing in the same way as an actor or an orator feels the presence of the audience.

D = Desire

Any reader who reads a book or a person who watches a film or a TV show, does so for one basic reason – desire. Why do people clap when the actor jumps off a tall building and remains unharmed? Why do they desire a beautiful actress? Why tears roll from the readers' eyes when an imaginary character of the novel deplorably fails in love or meets injustice? Why do they feel infuriated when a bad character exploits a child or inflicts harm on an innocent guy? Why do they want the villain to be crushed and the hero to be glorified? Because, through all these occurrences, <u>they want to see their own desires fulfilled</u>. When the actor jumps off a building and receives no injury, their own 'hidden desire' to be invincible and miraculous is satisfied. The beauty of the actress satiates their own inner appreciation of beauty. When the villain exploits an innocent fellow, it is their 'desire' to express kindness and justice that makes their blood boil.

Therefore, your writing must be capable of arousing a 'desired desire' in the hearts of the readers or the audience, in the same way as, when you are selling a pizza, it must be able to respond to the buyers 'desire' for taste and satisfaction. People will read your writing, when you press their desire veins. Think:

- How my writing is going to benefit people for whom it is written, so that they will desire to buy my book?
- What do they expect from such a book or writing?
- How far am I catering to these expectations?

- Am I giving them more than I am charging?

In consummating words, your writing must be so powerful that it evokes the <u>desire in the reader to buy</u> your book. If you are writing an advertisement, you must write the salient features of your product in a way that one desires to buy that product. If you are writing a project work, minutes or records, a report or web content, they should be so well written that your teacher, your boss, your manager or your client desires to read it with natural interest. When you write something from your heart, this quality comes effortlessly.

A = Action

As your readers wanted something from your book, you also must have wanted something from your readers – this is a reciprocal process.

For example, you are writing a book – **How To Increase Your Word Power**. Now, the people who would pick-up this book from a book-stall, when it is published, are surely people who have a 'desire' to increase their word power. On the other hand, your intention is to ensure that your readers are effectively able to enrich their vocabulary. To achieve this end, you might want some 'action' on the part of your readers. Give clear details of what activities the readers have to be involved in. If you want them to buy a certain book, advise them: *"For further details, please read my book 'Words and Their Roots', ABC Publishing House, New Delhi."* If you want them to visit a website, mention it: *"More information can be obtained from www.moreinformation.com."* Point out every action you want the readers to take to achieve what they 'desire'.

In advertisement copywriting, it means inducing the public to buy a specific product. For example: *"So, isn't the idea of getting a free air ticket to Singapore exciting? Wait no further! Rush to buy a mega box of* AppleCandy™ *chocolates and explore the magic before the stock finishes!"*

C = Caption

Caption plays the same role as does the signboard of a shop. If the signboard is 'attractive and descriptive', people will know what the shop offers and will feel invited. Your caption should also be *'attractive and descriptive'*. Choosing a good caption or title often leads to half of the success of a writing project. You might have written on a very nice theme, would have worked hard to put everything in order, the language and presentation might be impressive but if the caption is not appealing, nobody will even touch your book.

There are stories how a good book did not sell well and, later, the publisher just reprinted the book under a new title and it became a best-seller.

You must choose a 'sell-able' title for your write-up – unique but not queer, short, and summarizing the main purpose. Not only the title of the book but even sub-captions and chapter names inside the book should be given proper attention.

A = **Authenticity**

Once your book is published or your write-up exposed to people, you will be unable to make any changes. And remember the story of Picasso. Once he portrayed a picture and stuck it on the wall near the town square with the following note: "Please help me identify any shortcomings in the picture." Next day the whole drawing was full of red and black, blue and green pointers. There were so many errors in Picasso's work! The following day, Picasso stuck another copy of the same drawing with a note: "Please correct wherever there's an error." Next day he found the drawing untouched.

People will be very keen to find faults with your writing. Once your writing is exposed to thousand eyes, even some valid comments may come. You might have left some misinformation or misleading fact in your writing. You might not have mentioned the name of the copyright holder on an image or a text or you might have miscredited a quotation of Socrates to Plato or vise versa. Some facts you presented might be outdated and new findings must be something different.

It is also possible that you made historical or chronological errors. For example, it is possible that, in your writing, you are detailing a condition that happened 400 years ago and one of your characters is frequently using the word 'glasnost', though this word was mostly used by the Russian President Mikhail Gorbachev around 1980. And your another character, dating back before Newton, is talking about the Law of Gravity.

As a perfect writer you need to eliminate such inadvertent errors as they will badly destroy your image and mar the solidarity of your writing. Be very responsible in presenting the facts as authentically as you can. Shunning this responsibility will not only bring you down in the eyes of your readers but, in specific cases, may also drag you to legal suits.

So, do the needed research, ask concerned people, consult proper reference books, contact reliable sources and ensure that everything in your writing is unchallengeable, pure and authentic.

D = Depth

Your writing should bear weight and also have depth in it. You should write with grave intent and not shallow viewpoint. Books outlive kingdoms. So make sure that the futurity does not ever hold you as a trivial writer nor does it ridicule the shallowness of your childish ideas. Rather, as time passes, the gravity and profoundness of a writer should cause people to commemorate him. You must not be satisfied by giving superficial information. If you do so, there is no difference between you and a notice-board that gives only a stipulated piece of information. To be a writer, you need to develop your originality, describe something from your own point of view and prove to your readers that you are deeply and genuinely interested in providing them the required knowledge and necessary insight.

E = Empathy

As already discussed in *Chapter 5 (Observe and Imagine)*, Empathy is a quality of setting your feet in other's shoes. No matter you are writing a simple application to the Mayor of your City Council, a letter to your bosom friend or a more complex and detailed writing of any sort, the first thing you should do is to 'visualize' the reader who will read your creation. Imagine yourself in his or her place and think how a certain line, a paragraph, a word or a phrase will make him or her feel. If you honestly think that such an expression will hurt you, <u>don't write</u>. In just the preceding chapter you have already been advised to shun negative writing as it has a very short life and detrimental effect. Empathy ensures that you will not be involved in negative writing. To the contrary, if you feel that the given expression will stir up the needed impulse or feeling for the desired action, evoke kindness, attention, remedy, sympathy and help, <u>do write it</u>.

B = Beauty and Brevity

Beauty and brevity together make a balance. Focusing only on brevity at the cost of beauty may be good for some type of technical writing such as a medical prescription, price-list, product information, commodity labels, catalogues, listings, etc., but not for general writing. Brevity is something that comes after beauty. Beauty needs some details, and therefore too much brevity can kill it. On the other hand, too much of details will also make beauty like a fat, old woman and that is not a slim course. Therefore, a good writer walks making a balance between beauty and brevity.

R = Review/Revision

In the end, whatever is written deserves a revision. Usually, when you are writing, your focus is on your thoughts rather than on spellings and grammar. Especially, when you have written a big project – such as a book – it might have taken several months to complete that work. This long duration of time is, in itself, responsible for many errors. For example, you might have started the book in a Reporter style, using present tense, and by the third chapter your style changed into past tense. Apart from rectifying these missing uniformities, revision allows you to express your ideas more effectively, use better words, prune and curtail some over-repeated texts and add more charm to your writing.

No writing can be considered final and no writing – however carefully written – can claim to be flawless until it has been reviewed <u>at least once</u>, though preferably twice or thrice. Apart from other specifics related with your work, remember to check the following with due attention:

- Formatting
- Bullets and numbering
- Sub-captions and highlights
- Header and footer
- Bolds and italics (as necessary)
- Capitalization
- Punctuation

It will be helpful to read aloud your own writing. Almost all good writers have this habit, because when you read aloud, you assume the role of a 'reader' – more than of a writer – and are in a better position to evaluate your linguistic flow, audibility, phonetic effects, suitability of a word or a phrase as well as the overall impact and 'sound' of your written passages. Thus, you will be able to rectify many errors from the readers' point of view.

A = Acclimatization

'*Globalization*' and '*localization*' are two widely used terms these days, especially in the translation market. In this rapid wake of globalization, several big companies are expanding their markets all over the world. They launch their products and need to prepare advertisements, leaflets, product data, catalogues, websites, etc., – all in the language of the targeted population. '*Localization*' means developing these materials, based on the company's original stuff (often in English) using terms, styles, proverbs, jargons, punch lines, slogans, elements and ambience of the local market.

In other words, every person or agency involved in launching an international product has to '*acclimatize*' his writing campaign to appeal the local mass.

But '*acclimatization*' is not limited to translation and ad campaigns only. Every good writer, since the time when 'globalization' was not a word in dictionary, had taken care of 'acclimatization'.

When Walter De La Mare writes: "*You ... I thought you was in kitchen*", he is not committing a grammatical error by putting "*you was*" instead of "*you were*". Since the speaker is an illiterate servant, the poet is simply 'acclimatizing'. Thus 'acclimatizing' means 'tailoring' our writing according to place, time, character, and vogue ... and even to the specific need of a client or audience. It calls for natural flavors according to the demand of various circumstances within the writing.

Before finalizing your write-up, check it against this AIDACADEBRA formula and you will reap maximum benefits from your writing. So now take the rudder in your hands and sail freely, boldly and assuredly, in the vast ocean of the world of expressions! All the best!

Ten Top Tips

1. The first four letters of the magic formula for writers – AIDA – is already popular in the Advertisement world but they relate with all effective writing.

2. A writer's first duty is to draw the attention of his reader and then to maintain that attention throughout the writing.

3. The writing must be so powerful that it evokes the desire of the reader to buy the book or the product.

4. Choosing a good caption or title often leads to half of the success of a writing project.

5. Empathy ensures that we will not be involved in negative writing.

6. A good writer walks making a balance between beauty and brevity.

7. No writing can be considered final and flawless until it has been duly reviewed.

8. After finishing the writing, we must thoroughly check the formatting, bullets and numbering, header and footer, punctuation, etc. with due attention.

9. Reading aloud our own writing helps us to identify many errors from the readers' point of view.

10. 'Acclimatization' means 'tailoring' our writing according to place, time, character, and vogue … and even to the specific need of a client or audience.

Exercise 11

Match your answers with those given on the ANSWER PAGE. Give yourself 2 marks for each correct answer.

1. **Which step is <u>NOT</u> included in drawing the 'attention' of our reader?**
    A. Thinking who our readers are.
    B. Considering their time and climatic zone.
    C. Deciding what type of language should be used.
    D. Imagining how we can invite them into the subject.

2. **What type of language and style will be appropriate if we are preparing a power point material for training of junior managers of a motor vehicle company?**
    A. Childlike, humorous, light-hearted, very easy and funny language.
    B. Scientific, sober, full of examples, highly complex sentences.
    C. Interactive, technical, informative, simple and interesting language.
    D. Using technical jargons, compound sentences, scholarly language.

3. **Which one is a useful way to keep the reader 'interested' in our writing?**
    A. Make our writing interactive.
    B. Read our sentences aloud.
    C. Put a lot of humour in our writing.
    D. Write as briefly as we can.

4. **What will badly destroy your image and mar the solidarity of your writing?**
    A. Lack of beauty in your writing.
    B. Lack of depth in your writing.
    C. Not having a good caption or title.
    D. Lack of authenticity in your writing.

5. **A good writer should choose:**
    A. Beauty over brevity
    B. Brevity over beauty
    C. Beauty and brevity
    D. Neither beauty nor brevity

6. **What is <u>NOT</u> true about 'acclimatization'?**
    A. It is highly important in today's translation market.
    B. It gives authors some liberty for grammatical errors.
    C. It calls for natural flavors within the writing.
    D. It is to write suitably for a character or the audience.

Assignments 11

1. You are working in a private hospital. Your boss/manager is planning to sell out an old x-ray machine to make room for the MRI Unit. Write an ad for the potential buyers of the x-ray machine. (*Model answer given on ANSWER PAGE*)

2. Through the Internet, you have developed contacts with a small poor girl child of Ghana who is living in an orphanage. You are financially supporting that child. The girl has thanked you for your kind gesture and has sent you a small hand-made drawing to express her feelings. Now write back to the girl acknowledging her letter and appreciating the drawing she made. (*Model answer given on ANSWER PAGE*)

3. Punctuate the following passage and capitalize where necessary. (*Check your answer on the ANSWER PAGE*)

There was a carpenter who worked with a rich and noble master he used to make many 'items' for him then the carpenter became old and had to retire. The master called him and said now that you are leaving, I wish you do a last favour to me. What the carpenter asked as he was afraid that even till the end of his work-day, the 'cruel' master was not going to spare him. The master said, Just make a lovely wooden house i have to gift it to someone very special the reluctant carpenter spent many months after that, somehow dragging himself to complete the work and go and retire he did not care details. He did not invest the best of his talent. He could make a very nice and comfortable house but alas he did not do so. When the work was complete the master came to him and gave him a golden key and said: I wanted to gift this house to you, My great carpenter! You served me with such dedication! ...... Alas! It is too late being on the verge of death when we realize the generosity of our benevolent master, our God. If we knew that this ephemeral 'wooden house of soul' – this life - is truly his gift to us, we could invest more time and art, more attention and devotion in 'making' it into the Garden of Eden.

Two Prayers That Will Help You Write Well

A *prayer is a communication with our Greater Self. If said daily, in a spirit of devotion and expectancy, it gradually leaves a trail or mark on our subconscious mind. It attracts miraculous powers to wonder us. Read either or both these prayers – and ponder over their meaning - before going to bed and/or in the early morning, you'll feel the difference in a few months.*

1

O the Master of my mind!

O the Ruler of my heart!

O Thou Who releases every light,

every sound, smell and rhythm, in the right proportion!

Unleash my powers, unfasten my pen,

embolden my voice that I may express and promote

the beautiful truth and the true beauty.

I am nothing but an iota, yet a part of Thine effulgent Self –

more brilliant than a thousand suns.

Give me the capacity to touch the dust and turn it into gold.

Give me the power to enliven the dead and move the living.

May Your splendor alight on my writing,

Your majesty on my words,

and Your verve on my utterance.

O the Master of my mind!

O the Ruler of my heart!

2

Adorn my head, O God! My Lord!
With love for things that in this world
Are good and great and sweet indeed
And pure and beautiful, unsullied.

O God! My Lord! Just bless me so
Thou make me a lamp with love aglow
O God! Help fix my eyes on high
For a lofty cause let me live and die.

My blindness goes, I'm free from fear
My doubts dispelled, my vision is clear
My soul emboldened, my weakness shed
To such a world let me, O Lord! Be led.

ANSWER SECTION

ANSWERS TO EXERCISES

Exercise 1

1. C   2. D   3. A   4. D   5. B   6. D

Exercise 2

1. B   2. B   3. C   4. A   5. A   6. D

Exercise 3

1. C   2. A   3. B   4. A   5. D   6. C

Exercise 4

1. D   2. C   3. B   4. C   5. A   6. D

Exercise 5

1. B   2. D   3. A   4. D   5. C   6. A

Exercise 6

1. A   2. A   3. B   4. C   5. D   6. C

Exercise 7

1. D   2. C   3. A   4. A   5. B   6. C

Exercise 8

1. C   2. B   3. C   4. D   5. C   6. A

Exercise 9

1. C   2. C   3. B   4. D   5. B   6. A

Exercise 10

1. A 2. C 3. C 4. A 5. D 6. D

Exercise 11

1. B 2. C 3. A 4. D 5. C 6. B

WHAT IS YOUR OVERALL SCORE?

60-66 correct = **Excellent**   52-58 = **Very Good**

44-50 = **Good**   36-42 = **Satisfactory**

Chapter 9 : Answer to the Crossword Puzzle

G	L	O	R	Y			I		F
		O		C	A	N	O	E
		L				S		E
G	R	E	E	K		G	R	O	W	L
						M		
K	L	E	P	T	O	M	A	N	I	A
I		A		Y			I		M
T		R		S		B	A	R	B
T		R		T					E
E		O		E					R
N	E	A	T		R	O	B	I	N

ANSWERS TO ASSIGNMENTS
ASSIGNMENT 1

Ans 1.

Though I have been a voracious reader since my childhood, I think the most impressive book I've ever read is the ***Hidden Words of Bahá'u'lláh***. Those who haven't heard of Bahá'u'lláh or do not know his significance will surely appreciate his lofty station after reading the following comment of **Leo Tolstoy**, one of the greatest writers of all times: "***We spend our lives trying to unlock the mystery of the universe, but there was a Turkish prisoner, Bahá'u'lláh, in Akka, Palestine who had the key.***" Even though it is a very small book of 50-60 pages, one can spend about 50-60 years of his or her life trying to understand and implement even one verse of this great book. As Bahá'u'lláh has himself written, the ***Hidden Words*** is a summary and essence of all great teachings of world religions. Bahá'u'lláh is considered by his followers as the Messenger of God of this age. Those who do not want to believe in his manifestation as a prophet will find many pearls of wisdom in his ***Hidden Words***. He had excellent penmanship in Arabic and Persian and even the English translation (by Baha'u'llah's great grandson Shoghi Effendi) sounds so sublime that one may wonder how delightful and thought-provoking would it be to read the ***Hidden Words*** in its original form. The first half is originally in Arabic and the second half in Persian. **George TownsH**end, a noted writer, has thus expressed his impression about this book: "***The Hidden Words is a love-song. It has for its background the romance of all the ages—the Love of God and Man, of the Creator and His creature. Its theme is God's faithfulness and the unfaithfulness of Man***". He is true. It is a divine book that touches the core of every receptive reader's heart. Won't it be proper that I say nothing more about this book and just let you dive in the depth of this one passage from the ***Hidden Words*** and let you feel its sublimity by yourself: "***O People that have minds to know and ears to hear! The first call of the Beloved is this: O mystic nightingale! Abide not but in the rose-garden of the spirit. O messenger of the Solomon of love! Seek thou no shelter except in the Sheba of the well-beloved, and O immortal phoenix! dwell not save on the mount of faithfulness. Therein is thy habitation, if on the wings of thy soul thou soarest to the realm of the infinite and seekest to attain thy goal.***" [Words 424]

Ans 2.

My most favourite and 'Role Model' writer is Dr. Ramdhari Singh 'Dinkar' (23 September, 1908 – 24 April, 1974). 'Dinkar' was basically a Hindi poet but he also wrote a good volume of prose. I read his books "*Sanskriti Ke Chaar Adhyay*" and "*Sahityamukhi*". I was introduced with 'Dinkar' in my early childhood when my mother gave me to read an anthology of his poems – '*Renuka*'. As a poet he reflects a deep aesthetic sense, romanticism coupled with valor and, above all, a profound faith in the future of mankind. He was a poet of patriotic fervor and sang the song of India's glorious past and its bright future. Therefore, he was hailed as the 'Poet Laureate of India'. I learnt from 'Dinkar' that a man must be balanced in nature. He should not be so indulged in luxuries that his blood becomes cold. On the other hand, he must not be so dry-hearted that he forgets to worship the goddess of beauty. In his "composite philosophy" I found the reflection of Matthew Arnold's vision: "*He saw the life steadily and saw it whole*". I must admit that 'Dinkar' cast a spell on my teenage mind and became my 'Role Model' forever.

ASSIGNMENT 3

Ans 1.

(A) Larry Page and Sergey Brin   (B) E. O. Wilson   (C) David Hilbert   (D) Mahatma Gandhi   (E) Tolstoy   (F) Socrates   (G) Aryabhata   (H) William Hewlett and David Packard   (I) Plato   (J) Thomas Edison.

Give yourself 1 mark for each correct answer

Ans 2.

(A) Mark Twain   (B) Maharshi Vyas   (C) George Bernard Shaw   (D) Homer   (E) William Shakespeare

Give yourself 1 mark for each correct answer

ASSIGNMENT 4

Ans 1.

JOHN MILTON

John Milton was a noted English poet and writer. He was born in London on December 9, 1608. Interestingly, his father's name was also John Milton. He graduated from the University of Cambridge in 1629 and also acquired good knowledge of several languages including French, Greek, Hebrew, Italian, Latin and Spanish. No doubt, he was a well-studied person, noted for his profound knowledge. However, books were not the only source of his knowledge. He was also a widely travelled writer who undertook extensive tours to scores of places especially in Italy, France and Switzerland and met many prominent figures of his time including Galileo. Apart from being a poet and writer, John Milton was famous for his political views in support of Republican principles and he wrote extensively to propagate his political ideas. He used his pen to attack the church which was under the influence of the state. He wanted that the church must be free from, politics. Milton is also renowned for his philosophical thoughts on *Monism*. He believed and taught that everything in the universe – living or non-living – is made up of an *"animate, self-active, and free"* substance. His philosophical idea influenced many contemporary and posterior scholars. In 1643, he married Mary Powell who died in 1652. Mary's death was one of the most disturbing events of his life and then, two years later, he became blind. His best known poem – ***The Paradise Lost*** – was written in these catastrophic days of his life. Milton died on 8 November, 1674 abut he will always be remembered for his great intellectual contributions in the Restoration Period of European history. [270 words]

Ans 2.

1) L	2) M	3) O	4) I	5) E
6) C	7) A	8) G	9) F	10) D
11) J	12) K	13) N	14) H	15) B

Give yourself 1 mark for each correct answer

ASSIGNMENT 5

Ans 1.
I. Evening   II. Computer   III. Spider   IV. Hope   V. Friend

Give yourself 1 mark for each correct answer

Ans 2.
"Wherever the praises of God are sung, there verily is heaven".
– Guru Arjun Deo

31st July, 2010

Sardar Harkeerat Singh
7, Humdrum Street
A.D. Lane
Seattle (USA)

Dear Mr. Singh,

We were all in the village for over a fortnight and I am just back home while Dad is still there settling land dispute. I saw your express mail informing about the death of your beloved mother, Mrs. Sarabjeet Singh. I conveyed the news to my father on his cell phone and he joins me in expressing our deep felt grief.

Mrs. Singh was a valiant woman who took care of family after the death of your dear father, Sardar Gurcharan Singh, and left no stone unturned to nurture you as a most sacrificing parent. She stood as a light-house of guidance and courage for you and your brothers and paved the way for this prosperous business in Seattle that has eventually brought all fame and glory to your family. Her loss will be felt for ever but we all must take heart in this conviction that her inspiration will always be there to show us a brighter way.

We deeply regret that we could not take part in the Antim Ardas but our prayers surround her radiant soul. She was so pious and great-hearted that we earnestly believe her place is ever secured in Sachkhand, the Land of Eternal Truth and Light.

May God bless her with moksha!

Piyush Sharma
S/O Aditya Nath Sharma
Sindhi Colony
Gwalior (India)

ASSIGNMENT 6

Ans 3.

Constellation, galaxy, milky way, eclipse, sun, moon, stars, meteor, comet, cloud, space, black hole, horizon, solar system, Mars, Jupiter, Saturn, Mercury, nebula, ether.

ASSIGNMENT 7

Ans 1.

God could have programmed mankind to be essentially good and love Him. But that isn't the method of true love. Nobody wants a lover who is compelled to love unconsciously. Love is an emotional bond of mutual partnership and understanding. By giving "Free Will", God signed with each individual an agreement of love in which one has to choose Him voluntarily. God craves for our love and, in His own mystic ways, He encourages us to love Him without imposing any 'force' because if such a 'force' existed, there could be no meaning of 'free will'.

Original words = 285   After précis = 96

Answer Section 157

ASSIGNMENT 8

Ans 3.

(i)	=	(d)
(ii)	=	(a)
(iii)	=	(b)
(iv)	=	(f)
(v)	=	(h)
(vi)	=	(i)
(vii)	=	(e)
(viii)	=	(j)
(ix)	=	(g)
(x)	=	(c)

Give yourself 1 mark for each correct answer

ASSIGNMENT 9

Ans 2.

Column A	Column B
(i)	(e)
(ii)	(g)
(iii)	(h)
(iv)	(j)
(v)	(i)
(vi)	(h)
(vii)	(d)
(viii)	(b)
(ix)	(f)
(x)	(c)
(xi)	(a)

Give yourself 1 mark for each correct answer

Ans 3.

  (i) Foal
  (ii) Kitten
  (iii) Fawn
  (iv) Puppy
  (v) Tadpole
  (vi) Tod
  (vii) Leveret
  (viii) Colt
  (ix) Cub
  (x) Lamb
  (xi) Cygnet

Give yourself 1 mark for each correct answer

ASSIGNMENT 10

Ans 4.

To,

Joseph Carlos
Mayor
The City Council of Aidenburgh

Dear Mr. Carlos,

I feel concerned to let you know that for over a week the garbage collectors have not attended the area. As a result, the dustbins are lying in front of houses with nobody to lift them up. The intermittent rain has worsened the condition and the waste materials are not only stinking badly but are also contaminating drinking water sources.

  I wonder if the garbage collecting staff is on strike or there is some administrative oversight. However, I am sure that once the matter is brought to your attention, you will surely take some immediate measures to ensure cleanliness in this area. In fact, our trust in your green party which is ruling the council has been so strong that we know you are always more concerned than us for cleanliness and safety of the environment. That's why you enjoy the trust of people and are centre of their hope.

Your urgent attention to this matter will bring smiles to scores of faces.

Yours faithfully,

John Groan
Edmonton Cross

Ans 5.

(i)	=	(g)
(ii)	=	(d)
(iii)	=	(h)
(iv)	=	(j)
(v)	=	(i)
(vi)	=	(a)
(vii)	=	(b)
(viii)	=	(f)
(ix)	=	(e)
(x)	=	(c)

Give yourself 1 mark for each correct answer

ASSIGNMENT 11

Ans 1.

A 2 year old 300 MA Therapax BQ (Beam Quality) high frequency X-ray machine, ultra-modern technology is on sale at Starling Hospital, B.M. Road, to make room for extensive MRI Unit. This IS:7620 qualified X-ray machine is equipped with automatic safety system to block unwanted exposure factors beyond Tube Rating and Hand Switch with flexible long cord to keep the operator away from radiation area during exposure. To be sold on **FIRST COME FIRST SERVED** basis. Rush or call: 416 457 278.

Ans 2.

29th June, 2009

To,

Mamawa Swedel
Pious Church Poor Home
Victoria Crescent
Accra (Ghana)

Dear Mamawa,

Yesterday was my off day and I was in my garden looking at the freshest roses and remembering my lovely daughter, Tusharika, who is now in a boarding school in Panchgani (India). While I was missing her a lot, Jossi, my maid-servant silently came and gave me your letter which I kissed and opened immediately as I saw your name as the sender. I felt so happy to see that you sent me such a lovely and floral THANK YOU card but it was your drawing that touched my core even more deeply. To be truthful, I burst into tears as soon as I saw that heart-rendering portrait of a small girl half-opening the door andwith her sullen and searching eyes waiting for someone, as I understood it. I remembered my own childhood when I used to wait for the return of my mother from work.

Thank you for this pretty drawing. My dear Mamawa, I feel you have portrayed your own inner 'search' and depicted your patient waiting for the pleasant days to come. All that I can say is that, 'yes, you will see your golden days one day and will have as much delight on your face as are sparkles of the flowers in your greeting card'.

I welcome your sincere thanks and assure you that I have done nothing special. It is God who really deserves to be thanked and we are all just His humble instruments.

And now I want to give you a surprise! Next year, Tusharika, will be completing her schooling and will join me. After that, she and I have decided to fly to Ghana and bring you here from that orphanage. I had only one daughter ... but how grateful I am to God, I have now one more – you, Mamawa!

Eagerly awaiting till that time,
Yours affectionately,

Piyush R. Verman
N.R. Ray Street
Kolkata (India)

Ans 3.

There was a carpenter who worked with a rich and noble master. He used to make many 'items' for him. Then the carpenter became old and had to retire. The master called him and said, "Now that you are leaving, I wish you do a last favor to me". "What?" The carpenter asked as he was afraid that even till the end of his work-day, the 'cruel' master was not going to spare him. The master said, "Just make a lovely wooden house. I have to gift it to someone very special". The reluctant carpenter spent many months after that, somehow dragging himself to complete the work and go and retire. He did not care details. He did not invest the best of his arts. He could make a very nice, comfortable, beautiful and abiding house, but, alas! He did not do so. When the work was finished, the house was made, the master came to him, and giving him a golden key, said: "I wanted to gift this house to you, My great carpenter! You served me with such dedication!" .... Alas! It is too late, on the verge of death, when we realize the generosity of our benevolent Master, our God. If we knew that this ephemeral 'wooden house of soul' – this life - is truly His gift to us, we could invest more time and art, more attention and devotion in 'making' it into the Garden of Eden.

YOUR TOTAL SCORE ON THE ASSIGNMENTS
(Model Answers are not included)

Total marks for assignments = 75

WHAT IS YOUR OVERALL SCORE?

70-75 correct = **Excellent**   65-69 = **Good**

60-64 = **Fair**   55-59 = **Ok**

Heart-o-Meter

Answer all the questions **honestly** (*it means, tick mark only that which you really feel about yourself, not what you think is right or appropriate*) and follow the self-scoring pattern to know the level of your writing skill, now that you've completed reading this book.

Q 1. I agree that:
- ☐ A. I can write almost on any topic within a short notice.
- ☐ B. I can write almost on any topic if I am given few days' in to prepare.
- ☐ C. It is difficult for me to write on any topic, even if the topic is simple.
- ☐ D. I can never write easily on any topic.

Q 2. In my opinion, the most important thing for a successful writing is:
- ☐ A. Clear idea
- ☐ B. Right words
- ☐ C. Good sentences
- ☐ D. Style of writing

Q 3. Basically, true writing is:
- ☐ A. Something that should come from straight from the heart.
- ☐ B. Something which should reflect our intellect.
- ☐ C. Something which should be logical.
- ☐ D. Nonsense; it's the worst art of expression.

Q 4. My most favourite writer is the one who/whose:
- ☐ A. Books touch my heart and lead me to think something new.
- ☐ B. Teaches me new skills.

☐ C. Helps me enrich my vocabulary by putting new words in his contents.

☐ D. Books are always the best-sellers.

Q 5. Before I start writing:

☐ A. I calm my mind for a few minutes and imagine and then note down the basic outline of the subject.

☐ B. I think a little and start.

☐ C. I just think on the first line and start.

☐ D. I just start writing.

Q 6. In my opinion, a good writing normally has the following qualities in order of importance:

☐ A. Clarity, depth, beauty, brevity

☐ B. Depth, clarity, beauty, brevity

☐ C. Beauty, depth, clarity, brevity

☐ D. Brevity, beauty, depth, clarity

Q 7. When I have to write something:

☐ A. Words flow to me as I think and write.

☐ B. I sit with a dictionary and/or a thesaurus and choose the right words.

☐ C. I first write whatever comes and then rewrite everything in the end choosing the best words.

☐ D. I don't care for words. I just have to write somehow.

Q 8. I believe:

☐ A. In the power of my subconscious (inspirational) mind; it guides me through powerful writing.

☐ B. In the power of my conscious (logical) mind; it guides me through powerful writing.

☐ C. In good preparation on a vast range of topics; that's the key of success for a powerful writing.

☐ D. That there is nothing important about writing.

Q 9. I think that:

☐ A. I need to read a lots of good books to improve my writing.

☐ B. I need to read many books of my favourite writer to copy his or her style.

☐ C. Daily reading of newspaper is ideal for improving my writing.

☐ D. reading has nothing to do with my writing skill.

Q 10. I can write a 300 words paragraph on "The Goal Of My Life" in:

☐ A. about 10 minutes.

☐ B. about 15 minutes

☐ C. about 20 minutes

☐ D. I don't know

Now that you've honestly answered each question, score yourself as follows:
- For each '**A**' you have ticked, give yourself 4 marks.
- For each '**B**' you have ticked, give yourself 3 marks.
- For each '**C**' you have ticked, give yourself 2 marks.
- For each '**D**' you have ticked, give yourself 1 mark.

☐ 36-40 = **Very Good**   ☐ 32-35 = **Good**
☐ 28-31 = **Average**   ☐ Below 28 = **Poor**

Do you feel you have improved after completing this book? _____

Answer to the
Secret of the Secrets

They were all created

From the

Beginner's Guide To Journalism

Author: Barun Roy
Format: Paperback
Language: English
ISBN: 9788122306842
Code: 5621D
Pages: 124
Price: ₹ 150.00

Most books on journalism today are either too complex to comprehend or too superficial.

Barun Roy has really done a remarkably good job to fill a long-felt vacuum. This guide introduces basic tools of the applied journalism in simple language.

It provides step-by-step instructions to develop skills in the field. Any person interested in journalism, mass communication and in public relations will find this book very interesting, informative and useful.

It could even motivate you to contribute articles and features to newspapers and magazines as a freelance writer.

Some salient features of the book:
- What is journalism?
- News Gathering.
- News Lead.
- Putting the Story together.
- Writing in Newspaper Style.
- Colourful News Feature.
- Headline Story.
- Journalism as a Career.

Freelance Writing for the 'Newbie' Writer

Author: Sreelata Menon

Format: Paperback

Language: English

ISBN: 9788178061580

Code: 9367B

Pages: 132

Price: ₹ 150.00

*F*reelance Writing for the 'Newbie' Writer attempts to demystify the whole concept of creative freelance writing even while bringing out its pitfalls. The book highlights issues like importance of language, niche writing, querying an editor, reviewing a book, how to spot and avoid scams, plagiarism, and the requirements for publishing a book, etc.

It is essentially an introduction to the art of how to make your writing 'work' for you, as a newbie freelancer, needing to make a living out of it. The book does not tell you how to write. Instead, it tells you what to expect and what not to expect while you 'freelance' write.

Contents :

I - What Every Newbie Must Be Aware Of

II - What Every Newbie Must Acquire

III - What Every Newbie Must Know

IV - What Every Newbie Must Master

V - What Every Newbie Must Do

VI - Where Every Newbie Must Go

VII - What Every Newbie Must Follow

www.ingramcontent.com/pod-product-compliance
Lightning Source LLC
Chambersburg PA
CBHW070333230426
43663CB00011B/2301